SOLID TRUTH

Bible Studies for Postmodern Teens

Authors

Tom Couser, Mark Eiken, Kurt Mews, William Moorhead, Sara Pfeiffer
Jay Reed, Greg Rommel, Matt Schaefer, Joel Symmank

DCE Korey Danley's
Library

CPH
Concordia Publishing House

Editor

Tom Nummela

Your comments and suggestions concerning the material are appreciated. Please write the Product Manager, Youth Bible Studies, Concordia Publishing House, 3558 S. Jefferson Avenue, St. Louis, MO 63118-3968.

Scripture taken from the HOLY BIBLE, NEW INTERNATIONAL VERSION®. NIV®. Copyright © 1973, 1978, 1984 by International Bible Society. Used by permission of Zondervan Publishing House. All rights reserved.

Copyright © 1998 Concordia Publishing House
3558 S. Jefferson Avenue, St. Louis, MO 63118-3968
Manufactured in the United States of America

1   2   3   4   5   6   7   8   9   10   07   06   05   04   03   02   01   00   99   98

Contents

... in the Holy Spirit (The Third Article)

Introduction

About Solid Truth

These studies are directed at a new generation of teenagers. Today's high school students are growing up in a world in the midst of change. A new worldview challenges many of the basic assumptions of the generations that preceded them. A new way of thinking surrounds them, influencing their education, entertainment, music, and, in turn, their approach to life. These are postmodern times.

The nature of postmodernism is discussed more fully later in this introduction. It shows itself in the lives of young people in a rejection of absolute truth, a high tolerance for diversity, and a high level of technological savvy and worldliness. It creates a kind of moral, philosophical, and spiritual quicksand. It can make leading Bible study with these young people a real challenge.

These 12 Bible studies tackle the issues raised by postmodernism head-on, using relational techniques that will appeal to today's relational teens. The topics are drawn from the real-life challenges of living as a Christian in a postmodern world. They are organized around the Apostles' Creed. The Creed proves to be an effective means to communicate the *Solid Truth* of God's Word to postmodern teens.

> **Postmodernism creates a kind of moral, philosophical, and spiritual quicksand.**

This is not primarily a course on the Apostles' Creed, however. It is a set of in-depth *Bible* studies on the basic truths of the Christian faith. It can be used as a review of those basic teachings, but the studies will also challenge both mature Christian young people and new Bible students to look deeply and seriously at God's Word of truth.

Postmodern Thought

We live in an age of diversity. Our once rather monolithic culture is rapidly becoming a stew of nationalities and cultures, in which each ingredient retains its particular flavor and texture even as it is mingled with many others. The result is no longer the "melting pot" some envisioned, but a multicultural challenge of significant proportions. The church is fully equipped through God's Word to meet this challenge—but are the equippers up to it?

What is more alarming, however, is that there is an even greater cultural challenge facing us—a cultural shift such as may not have been seen since the Enlightenment and the beginning of the so-called modern era. Many scholars suggest that we are seeing the end of modernity and the beginning of the postmodern era, a shift in worldview that will affect all corners of our society—including, and perhaps most significantly, the church.

In postmodernity we are witnessing the end of humanity's dream that reason, human intelligence, and scientific advancement would bring about dramatic, lasting solutions to society's problems. A new social mindset is at work in the children and grandchildren of the Baby Boom generation. The young people we deal with in the church today and in the future will be more unlike their parents and grandparents than ever before. They represent one of the biggest challenges that the church has had to face.

The crisis is one of culture. How can we as a church communicate the Gospel effectively to Generation X and their younger siblings in the "millennial" generation—the first generations of the postmodern times? The need is urgent, for if the shift in worldview is as great as contemporary prophets claim, our current approaches and tools will not suffice. Significant portions of these new generations will not automatically share the faith of their parents and grandparents. Many mainline denominations could continue to decline and some might cease to exist. The church itself will be at risk, for it is true that in matters of faith, each individual—each generation—must come to faith personally. "God has no grand-children."

Postmodern thought will bring many challenges to the church's ministry over the next 20 years—initially with teenagers and young adults, but increasingly in all areas of the church's work. It is self-evident that at some point in the future, the church will be populated by people living in, and culturally attuned to, the postmodern age. We seek the resources God provides His church to address issues in every age.

The Challenge of Postmodernity

As part of God's ongoing creation, people and the world in which we live continue to change, develop, and grow. From the beginning of time, we have accumulated knowledge about the world and all the things in it—all as gifts from God. This body of knowledge has not always been a blessing. It has resulted in awesome capacity for nuclear destruction, occasional environmental catastrophe, and medical technology that tempts us to once again seek equality with God. At times this growth in knowledge has resulted in sweeping changes in our worldview—the way in which we address ourselves to the world.

> **If the shift in worldview is as great as contemporary prophets claim, our current approaches and tools will not suffice.**

The Renaissance was one such sweeping change. With the invention of moveable type and the Gutenberg press, information could be rapidly and broadly shared. The communications explosion that resulted gave a powerful boost to the Reformation and brought an end to the age when information was primarily transmitted orally.

This shift into the modern era was dramatic. Society moved from an agrarian society to one based on industry. The "size of the world" increased enormously, from a few square miles in the local fiefdom for the vast majority of people to a concept of "nation" and eventual colonization of the globe. The serf/master relationship gave way to a growing emphasis on individual autonomy and freedom.

An equally significant shift is taking place today, the beginning of the postmodern age. In some ways it is a return to oral communication. It is powered not by the printing press (nor by engines run by steam, internal combustion, nor even atomic fission), but by a combination of video technology, computer science, and telecommunications that has changed forever the way we think and interact on this planet.

Tim Celek, pastor of a large, young congregation in southern California, shared the characteristic differences between modernism and postmodernism at a youth workers conference in January 1997; the conference was titled "Youth Ministry toward 2000." Some of his thoughts are grouped here under three categories.

Their Perceptions of the World

- The modern era saw technology as a means of liberation; postmodernism uses technology for entertainment.
- The modern era was based largely on growth in industry; postmodernism is based on the growth of information.
- The modern era sought to conquer the earth; postmodernism is concerned with cooperating with the environment.
- The modern era's preoccupation with nationalism and colonialism is giving way to postmodernity's emphasis on globalization and multiculturalism.

Anthropological Perspectives

- The modern era held as an ideal the autonomous self; postmodernism stresses community and dependence.
- The modern era believed in the inherent goodness of man; postmodernism recognizes man's "sinfulness"—our inability to do and be good.
- The modern era emphasized reason; postmodernism emphasizes experience.
- The modern era focused on the head and intellect; postmodernism focuses on the heart and the will.

Individual Focus

- The modern era tended to be future-oriented; postmodernism will be present-oriented.
- Where the modern era was idealistic and optimistic, postmodernism will tend to pragmatism and cynicism.
- The modern person sought to be relevant; the postmodern person values being real.
- The modern era resulted in fundamentalists; postmodernism will see relativists.
- The modern era recognized individual responsibility; postmodernism tends to focus on collective responsibility.

In the modern era boundaries were strong. People had a sense of place and of what was expected of them in that place. Loyalties were strong and people identified themselves by membership in community, vocation, and family. With boundaries strong, the need for individual vision was not great. In the postmodern age, we are seeing the falling away of boundaries of all kinds—family structure, political and geographic isolation, moral expectations, and denominational loyalty. The need for this age will be a strong vision—a personally held understanding of the purpose and value of each association and activity. It may be that the church has a chance at providing just such a vision. This book is one step in that direction.

Postmodernity can be seen as a confluence of generational changes, social realities such as family structure, and historical "progress," especially in technology and communication. These forces have all contributed to the shift to a postmodern worldview.

Family changes—more single parents, high divorce rate, children having children, and dual income households—are also well-documented. Some suggest that nearly 50 percent of these generations will experience the divorce of their parents, some more than once. They face three times the risk of a broken home as their grandparents. These are generations that have been "home alone"; the term latch-key was popularized for them. They are *The Hurried Child* of David Elkind's book. Many have a sense of having raised themselves. The result is that they hunger for, but at times also avoid, relationships.

Thanks to technology, we are truly becoming part of a global village. We see instantly things that happen on the other side of our world and talk intimately with friends in the next room, the next house, the next country, or on the next continent. The citizens of this new age are different in striking ways from the people who have comprised the majority in our churches in the past century or more. If we hope to share the Gospel with the younger members of this world community, we will need to recognize and address ourselves to the many ways in which they are different, even as we affirm the many ways they are like us.

Generational Differences

The striking differences between the members of successive generations is a large part of this postmodern shift. Recognizing these differences and adjusting our ministry styles accordingly will allow us to minister more effectively to postmodern teens. Most experts recognize four significantly different generations in the United States today— Builders, Boomers, Busters, and the Millennial Generation.

1. The "Builders" or "Boosters" were for the most part born before 1945. They were shaped by two world wars and the Great Depression. "Key issues of safety, security, and stability have been reflected in their conservatism and belief in the values of institutions." (The concepts here and in the next two paragraphs are drawn from *NetFax: Helping Church Leaders Make the Transition from the Present to the Future* [Tyler, TX: Leadership Network, January 22, 1996], and used by permission. *NetFax* is a bi-weekly, one-page fax transmitted to an open sub-

scription list.) Their favorite pronoun could be said to be *we,* for they have consistently worked for the good of the whole. You may frequently hear a member of this generation say "No sweat!" but they have worked hard all their lives.

2. The "Boomers" are a widely studied generation, usually taken to be those born between 1945 and 1965. "The 76 million Boomers have been shaped by the significant social and political changes of the 60s and 70s, the shift to a consumer culture, and music/media. Indulged by their parents and a culture that has responded to each new stage of their life, these searchers and seekers have been on lifelong journeys of discovery" (*NetFax,* 1/22/96). Facing key issues of identity, meaning, and personal growth, Boomers have frequently been called the "*Me* generation"; their goal has been self-fulfillment. Boomers may frequently say "No problem," but they have faced all kinds of problems and anxieties in their lives.

3. The "Busters" (so-called because the birthrate that impelled the "Boomers" to great numbers went "bust" for this generation) is generally said to be those born between 1965 and 1985. "The first postmodern generation, Busters have been shaped by the emergence of a global economy, the end of the Cold War, revolution in information and technology, dysfunctional families, environmental problems, and crises of addictions, AIDS, violence, and no absolutes to name just four" (*NetFax,* 1/22/96). The Busters, also called Generation X, are also looking for identity, but most frequently find it in relationships and the community of their peers. Their pronoun of choice then is *us.* Their slogan is borrowed from a national sports apparel advertising campaign—"No fear"—but they have significant fears about what the future holds.

> **Recognizing generational differences, and adjusting our ministry styles accordingly, will allow us to minister more effectively to postmodern teens.**

4. The Millennial Generation (it includes the "millennial" high school graduating class of 2000) consists of those born after 1985. This generation is truly at home with media and technology. They have been raised with video cameras and computers close at hand, frequently finding "community" even in their electronic world. This is a fast-paced generation, raised on "sound bites" and 10-second commercials with the remote control in hand. They are largely jaded with experience and information overload, cynical (remember they grew up on the media), and highly oriented to the present. You may hear their refrain, "Been there, done that," and realize how difficult they might be to really impress.

These last two generations—Generation X and the Millennials—are observably influenced by the postmodern trends described in the previous section.

The characteristics of Generation X (those currently aged 15 to 35) have been widely reported: they exhibit a strong self-reliance, face a declining standard of living, wrestle with relevance of education and career choices, stress the importance of family and friends, employ technology readily, demonstrate attitudes of toleration and altruism, and seek spiritual experiences (but not always Christian ones).

The characteristics of the "Millennials" (those under age 15) who are just now entering our youth ministry programs are less widely known—at least in part because their story is just now being written. They are portrayed in the media as likeable and self-reliant (remember *Home Alone?*), they are sophisticated consumers, very now-oriented, at home with computer technology, and expect life to be fast-paced and nonlinear. These new generations differ in significant ways from the generations that preceded them, the Builders (those who are currently 55-75 years old) and the Baby Boom generation (currently about 35-55 years of age).

Many of those who teach and lead youth Bible classes are likely to be Baby Boomers. Yet we have the challenge to reach out to Generation X and those that follow. There are inevitable conflicts that will result from these differences. Our ability to communicate across generational lines during Bible classes and the like will improve as we learn to keep these generational differences in mind.

Leading Bible Study for Postmodern Teens

The differences in the worldview now and 20 years from now are dramatic and troublesome for a church whose goal is to continue to reach out to the world—the postmodern world—with the Good News of Jesus Christ. The problem is not just a generational difference, but a changing worldview and a different culture between those under the age of 35 and those over that age.

Nor are the problems just temporary. Generation X and their Millennial siblings are not going to "grow up." From the perspective of their parents and grandparents, the young adults in Generation X may appear immature or childish. Many older adults cling to the hope that these young adults will at some time in the near future grow up, change to be more like their Boomer and Builder forbears. But if the differences as we have described them are truly generational, cultural, and inherent in the philosophical starting place for these young adults, they are not likely to change magically. These young people may be forced to accommodate themselves to the perspectives of their elders in order to hold a desired job or live at home with their parents, but their basic worldview will not change. They may simply avoid voluntary relationships with a church that does not understand them and does not seek to reach them "as they are."

What can we do? The first step is to acknowledge that we may be in need of new tools, new ideas, new ways of doing things in youth ministry. Though God's truth doesn't change, we can learn new ways to apply it. We need to recognize this need to learn. Eric Hoffer says it well:

> In times of change, *the Learners* inherit the earth, while *the Learned* find themselves beautifully equipped to deal with a world that no longer exists.

(From *Next,* April 1996, page 16)

Once we have accepted the concept that our current frustration with ministry to young adults and youth is due at least in part to a difference in worldview—the result of shifting culture—then we have a clue as to where we might seek answers to improving our skill in sharing the Gospel with these new generations. Rather than insisting on a *status quo* that results in "culture wars" between generations or the passive departure of future generations from the church, we can learn to minister to them cross-culturally. Such cross-cultural communication of the Gospel is nothing new. It has been taking place for nearly 2,000 years since the apostle Paul and his fellow missionaries began to reach out beyond the narrow confines of Judea with the message of Christ. The experiences of those who have ministered cross-culturally provide helpful insights into the strategies and techniques that will reach culturally distinct generations of youth and young adults.

1. Be willing to immerse yourself in the new culture. As we reach out to postmodern young people, it will be impractical to expect that they will step out of their culture and adopt the mindset of older generations. It is our responsibility to *bring* the message of the Gospel and communicate it to them.

2. Listen to the music and observe the art of the culture. As we have seen Generation X and the Millennial generation described, it is clear that art—especially music—will prove a useful field of study. The art of the postmodern generations is easy to find on prime-time television, in the local movie theater, and booming from the local top 40 radio station.

3. Expect "cultural idolatry"—the notion that *my* culture is superior to your culture and you should adopt mine. We all tend to evaluate every culture from our own perspective and against our own cultural norms. Such an approach will create barriers between us and the culture we seek to reach. At the same time, remember that no culture is perfect—ours or anyone else's. Every human culture is subject to the problem of sin. Where the tenets of postmodernism run counter to God's Word, we cling to His Word of truth and make our case for it in as persuasive a way as possible.

4. Recognize cultural diversity as a blessing, not a curse. This basic truth, expressed vividly in Paul's first letter to the Corinthians, chapter 12, can assist us greatly in overcoming the gaps between modern and postmodern thinkers in our churches. We can affirm, and help young adults to affirm, the tremendous contributions of the Builders and Boomers to the church, the importance of their leadership, and the many ways in which they serve. We can also affirm, and help older adults to affirm, the tremendous gifts and strengths that the young adults and youth of the church possess and we can stress the importance of "making room" for them in the structure and ministry of the church.

5. We can build cultural bridges between the modern and postmodern thinkers in our congregations by creating opportunities for the Builder and Boomer leaders in our churches and youth-ministry programs to experience youth culture in nonthreatening ways—showing film clips and television excerpts that reveal postmodern values and reminding the viewers of the social events that have shaped those values; sharing lyrics from popular music recordings of the new generations and addressing the positive and negative issues they reveal; with other adults, visiting the places that young adults assemble for recreation and observe closely the depth of the relationships and the topics of their conversations.

Servant events, where young adults and older adults work and sweat together side by side for a common purpose, are great bridges to understanding and appreciating one another. Joint opportunities for worship and recreation will help as well. And while marriage is not a practical strategy, its inclusion on the list is a reminder that building one-on-one partnerships or mentoring relationships between the young and old remains a powerful tool for helping both individuals to grow and bond.

6. Mentor and equip "indigenous" ministers. This strategy has had strong success in the foreign mission fields. It suggests the powerful influence possible when even just a few young adults can be built up as leaders in ministry to their peers. The strong relationships among these younger generations will make relational evangelism and peer ministry bear tremendous fruit.

7. Use their tools in your ministry. The computer is a fact of life for most members of the postmodern generations. High percentages of them are on line daily, visiting sites on the Internet and connecting with friends (locally and internationally) through electronic mail and on-line chat-rooms (real time, typed conversations among as many as a dozen or more individuals). Such computer-based tools represent a powerful way for the church to connect with young people and stay connected with them through departure to college, career and job changes, and cross-country, or international relocation.

The postmodern media provide other tools that can be put to work by the church. Staged news events, television shows about television shows, real-life police and paramedic dramas, and programs featuring home videos are just a few of the offerings popular among postmodern young people. Such shows feature a carefully edited, frequently nonlinear, always dynamic version of reality—the boring parts of reality have been removed. It can be productive to engage young people in discussion about this kind of media. "Why is it interesting? Is it 'real'? What does it reveal about us?"

8. Christian truth is counter-cultural, but also cross-cultural and supra-cultural. It has relevance for all time. Certainly parts of the Christian truth run counter to the sinful parts of every culture. But the basic appeal of the Good News is relevant for all cultures. And it offers hope for the postmodern teen who, without Christ, sees a bleak present and nothing better in his future.

9. Recognize the distinction between "text" (the divine truth of God's Word) and "the context" (the form, setting, language, and interpretation of that Word). We must learn to communicate the "unchanging truth" in and to a "changing world."

To be effective our presentation of that truth should have at least four characteristics.

1. Honesty. Postmodern teens are keenly attuned to exaggeration and false fronts. The effective leader will be open and vulnerable, sharing from the heart a message that is personal and real.

2. Energy. Genuine enthusiasm for the teaching task and evident interest in the students will go a long way in maintaining student interest and participation.

3. Relevance. These young people are looking for the practical application of the spiritual truths they are asked to accept and learn. Expect to spend at least a third of each class session applying God's Word in ways that the students see will make a difference in their lives.

4. Relationships. These are generations who live for relationships with their peers. Use peer discussion groups, especially in larger classes, allowing the students to interact with each other as they discuss and apply the lesson truths. Make frequent application to the relationships they have with close friends and acquaintances. Spend time getting to know them and letting them get to know you.

In these ways we can communicate the truth (the text) in a way that it will be heard (the context) so that the hearer can truly benefit from our message.

To the extent that we can learn to do those things—to the extent we are learners, people who know they are on the way to improved ministry to new generations, rather than learned, people who believe they have already arrived at the only way to communicate God's truth—we will increase our effectiveness in

> **Where the tenets of postmodernism run counter to God's Word, we cling to His Word of truth and make our case for it in as persuasive a way as possible.**

communicating the Gospel message, according to God's grace. Then we can share the Gospel with today's young people, despite the challenges of postmodernity and all that it represents.

Creeds and Confessions

Since the earliest days of the church, Christians have employed credal statements to confess their Spirit-given faith in the truth of God's Word. Peter's confession in Matthew 16, "You are the Christ," and Paul's admonition, "No one can say, 'Jesus is Lord' except by the Holy Spirit" (1 Corinthians 12:3), are but two examples. In time, these brief exhortations were developed into longer summaries of the principal teachings of the Christian faith. In this volume the Apostles' Creed has been used as the organizing principle for the studies. It is chosen for its great simplicity. The Nicene Creed is similar in content and structure and could have served well also.

In its present form, the Apostles' Creed dates from the eighth century. It is a revision of an earlier creed often called the Old Roman Creed that was used as early as the third century. It draws its title as a statement of the apostles' teachings, though its writing cannot be traced to the apostles themselves.

The creeds have served in two significant ways. First, they have been teaching tools for educating those new to the Christian faith in its basics. Then also, in times of struggle, Christians have turned to the creeds of the church, especially the Apostles' Creed and the Nicene Creed, to reaffirm and renew their faith when the truth of God's Word was contested by those inside or outside the church.

It is appropriate then that we return to the creeds in these early years of the postmodern era to renew and refresh our faith and reacquaint ourselves with the basic teachings upon which the church was built over the centuries. There we find the clear teachings of Scripture stated in an orderly way. They are teachings that have changed the lives of millions of people in the past 2,000 years. They remain the basic foundations of the Christian faith, God's solid truth.

The Apostles' Creed

First Article

I believe in God, the Father Almighty, Maker of heaven and earth.

Second Article

[I believe] in Jesus Christ, His only Son, our Lord, who was conceived by the Holy Spirit, born of the Virgin Mary, suffered under Pontius Pilate, was crucified, died and was buried. He descended into hell. The third day He rose again from the dead. He ascended into heaven and sits at the right hand of God, the Father Almighty. From thence He will come to judge the living and the dead.

Third Article

I believe in the Holy Spirit, the holy Christian church, the communion of saints, the forgiveness of sins, the resurrection of the body, and the life everlasting. Amen.

The Creed is, at its heart, a summary of Christian faith—a story with three characters, all of whom are God, and a plot that seeks to capture the key thoughts of the Holy Scriptures. It is not a system of doctrine but a statement of truth—the *solid truth* of God's Word. The first two studies in this book establish the background of this statement of truth: (1) how God reveals Himself to His people, especially through His Word, and (2) the triune nature of God who reveals Himself to us as Father, Son, and Holy Spirit.

Solid Truth

John 14:1–14, especially 9–14

Study Outline

Activity	Time Suggested	Materials Needed
Opening Activity (Choose 1)		
How Do You Know ...?	10 minutes	Marker board or newsprint and markers
Learning to Love	10 minutes	
Studying the Word		
Natural Knowledge of God	10 minutes	Copies of Resource Page 1A; pencils or pens; Bibles
Revealed Knowledge of God	10 minutes	Copies of Resource Page 1B; pencils or pens; Bibles
Applying the Word		
Weigh the Evidence	10 minutes	Newsprint or marker board and markers
(Optional) Just the Facts	10 minutes	Copies of Resource Page 1C; pencils or pens
Closing Prayer	10 minutes	Index cards; pencils or pens

Opening Activity

Choose one—but not both—of the following activities, unless you have extra time.

How Do You Know ...?

On a marker board or large sheet of newsprint write "How do you know ...?" When your students have arrived, direct them into pairs or groups of three. Invite them to share with their group things they know about (1) their great grandparents, (2) Abraham Lincoln, or (3) their favorite athlete or entertainer. Limit each person to two minutes. Then gather the students into one group and ask, "How do you know what you know about the person or people you described?" They will likely cite credible sources such as relatives' eyewitness accounts, stories passed down through the family, historical documents, textbooks, or newspapers and other media. Point out that they learn nearly everything in their lives from two kinds of sources—personal experience or information from others.

Then ask, "What about God? How do you know things about Him?" Invite volunteers to share their thoughts. Encourage other students to ask questions and suggest responses.

After about five minutes, conclude by saying, "The existence of God has

Focus

Postmodern thinking denies the possibility of certainty. It undermines notions of truth and authority. This leaves many young people today sinking in postmodern "quicksand." We can introduce them to a God who seeks us out and offers us sure knowledge of His existence and His love. God's existence can be seen in creation, in His continued work in the world, and in the Law written on our hearts (the "natural" knowledge of God). His love can be seen only in the solid truth of His written Word, the Bible, as it reveals the Good News of salvation through His Son, the Word made flesh (the "Christian" or revealed knowledge of God).

Objectives

Through the power of God's Word, students will

1. distinguish between the natural and revealed knowledge of God;
2. by faith, acknowledge the truth of God's Word through which God reveals Himself;
3. rejoice that God seeks us and reveals Himself to us.

For a longer study:
Arrange for two teams to debate each other. One team will try to prove that there is no God. The other will argue that He not only exists, but has made Himself known to humanity. Allow each team to prepare for a few minutes. Assign a few students or adult leaders as judges to decide which team was more convincing.

been debated all through history. It's a good question, one that a lot of people are asking. Today we want to answer the question, 'How do you know there is a God, and how can you tell what He's like?'—for ourselves and for the times when others ask that question of us."

Or ...

Choose this activity or the previous one, but not both unless you have extra time.

Learning to Love

Share this background information: In some cultures, people unite as husband and wife through *arranged* marriages. At an early age they are promised to one another by their parents. When the appropriate age is reached, the couple begins a courting relationship that is expected to lead to marriage. It might seem strange to us, because we want to see, know about, and approve of the person we are going to marry. We fear getting stuck with a dud.

Ask, "How might you try to determine if a person is the *right one* for you?" Possible responses include learning about them; getting the *facts* (what they like, what they look like, their habits); spending time together; or developing a relationship.

Conventional wisdom might say, "You wouldn't really know if he or she is *the one* until you experience a relationship. You'd better check things out before you commit to a lifelong arrangement." But some people get caught up in dating a bunch of people and never settle on *one.* They never know the joy of a committed, lifelong relationship. Instead, they invest in many consecutive or simultaneous relationships and endure great emotional pain when those relationships end.

Next ask, "Suppose that you were guaranteed that an arranged marriage would be the best marriage possible for you. Would you go for it?" Allow a moment for students to share their responses.

Conclude by saying, "When it comes to God, we have that kind of guarantee. God chooses us with a powerful, lifelong love. But we don't go into our relationship with God totally blind. He has given us ways to know Him. He brings us into a relationship with Him so that we will know, firsthand, of His love and goodness. Today we will look at how God reveals Himself to us—gives us knowledge about Himself—and how we experience His love and presence in our lives."

Studying the Word

Use both of these activities.

Natural Knowledge of God

Explain to your students, "No matter how much *proof* is given for the existence of God (archaeological evidence, historical documents, biblical accounts, reasoned arguments, personal experience), there is one necessary element for anyone to know God: faith. In John 6:44 Jesus said, 'No one can come to Me unless the Father who sent Me draws him.' Our relationship with God and His Son Jesus Christ, and the eternal life God provides are not a matter of knowledge, but of faith. This is the gift given to us by God through the Holy Spirit. In response to our faith, God calls us, as 1 Peter 3:15 points out, to 'Always be prepared to give an answer to everyone who asks you to give the reason for the hope that you have.' God wants us to be able to give a reasoned answer, not to say, 'Well, you just have to believe,' but to help people know what to believe and why. This includes not only the basic facts of the Gospel but also testifying to how God is at work in our lives and in the world around us.

"But what can we tell others about God? What can we know about Him? The Scriptures say that God has made Himself known in three ways." Distribute copies of Resource Page 1A, "Natural Knowledge of God," to the students. Direct the students to read the three Bible passages and complete the sentence "We know Him by …" for each. After about five minutes, invite volunteers to share their work. Suggested responses are Psalm 19:1-6—creation, what God has made; Romans 2:14-15—our conscience; John 20:31—His Word, the Bible.

The first two ways God reveals Himself are called *natural* knowledge, that is, God showing Himself through what He has made. We can learn certain things about what God is like by observing nature. Ask, "What qualities of God are revealed in the following parts of nature?" (Suggested answers are in parentheses.)

- the cycle of evaporation and rain (God is provider)
- the seasons of the year (God is intentional, He plans)
- the intricacy of a hummingbird (God is detailed)
- the stars and planets out in space (God is infinite)
- the variety in the human species (God is creative and values individuality)
- the Grand Canyon or a spectacular sunset (God is majestic)

Revealed Knowledge of God

Ask, "Why is it that some people see all these marvels of creation but don't see the Creator behind them?" (They do not have faith in God. Romans 1:20-21 says that people became foolish in their thinking and chose to ignore God.)

Through creation God reveals Himself to us in a general way. But the specifics of God are not revealed by nature. For instance, what His name is and what His purposes are, how He wants people to know Him, and how much He loves each person—these are all known through *revealed* knowledge of God.

Revealed knowledge comes to us through His Word, the Bible (see John 1:1, 14; Hebrews 1:1-2). Through nature God says to us "I exist." Through revealed knowledge, His Word, He tells us what He has done

19

for us, that He is present right now, and how we are to live in relationship to Him.

Romans 1:20 tells us that no one will be able to say "I didn't know there was a God," because God has made His presence plain to all people through the testimony of what He has made. But God doesn't want people just to know He exists, then wander around trying to guess what He's about.

Challenge the students by saying, "Suppose a skeptic friend says to you, 'Okay, so there's a Creator. How can you know what He's like? How do you know that He loves you?' What do you say?" Give them a few minutes to think about the question. Then distribute copies of Resource Page 1B. Unless your class is small, direct the students to discuss the questions in small groups. Then review them with the whole class.

In the second section of the page, emphasize that when Jesus says, *I am the way, truth, and life"* He points His followers to Himself. Underscore that all of Scripture points to Christ and the salvation He earned for us at Calvary.

The students' summary of Jesus' message might read, "If you've seen Me, you've seen God." We know God by knowing Jesus.

Conclude this activity by saying, "You can come to know what God is like based on the evidence—the work of His hands in creation and the life of His Son as revealed in the Scriptures. Ephesians 2:8 says that we receive grace, the saving knowledge of God, through faith and that both are a gift of God. God is not a hidden mystery. He gives the ability to *see* Him, to know Him, as a free gift. We know that there is a God, and we know a few things about this God as He reveals Himself to us through what He has made. We also know Him because He has 'written His law on our hearts,' in our consciences. But we can only know Him—who He is, how He has saved us from sin and given us new life—through a relationship with Jesus. And that knowledge comes by faith, as we grow in our knowledge of the word of God and live by faith according to His ways (Romans 10:17)."

Applying the Word
Weigh the Evidence

On the board or newsprint write at the top on one side "Evidence from the Word" and at the top on the other side, "Evidence around Us." Ask, "What are things about God that would be important for someone to know who is not a Christian? What are the most important things the Bible says about who God is and what He has done?"

Under the "Word" heading, make a list of the things they share. (God created the world, including all people. He spoke to us through the Word, loves us, sent Jesus to die for our sins, promises to be with us always and will come again to judge the world. The Apostles' Creed is an excellent outline of the basic facts of the Scriptures.)

Next ask, "In what ways do you see God's hand in your lives and the world around you?" Write their responses in the other column. (Loving relationships, the church, specific instances of healing, strength and encouragement in their lives.) Then say, "God's Word establishes the facts of our faith. If we want to know God, we must know Him through the person of Jesus Christ as revealed to us through His Word. We know and *see* God in our lives and the world around us as we grow in His Word and as He shows us His hand working in us, through us, and around us."

Just the Facts

Use this activity only if you have extra time.

If your students are interested in a rational approach to how we know about God, work through Resource Page 1C. Explain that having a rational, logical approach to knowing God does not bring about faith, but it can help decrease someone's resistance to looking at the Word to see what it says. This outline is simply an ordered approach to why believing in Jesus makes sense.

Closing Prayer

Distribute index cards. On one side, ask your students to write a one-sentence prayer of thanks for a way that God has revealed Himself to them. Remind them of some of the ways you have discussed—through creation, the Law written on our hearts, the Word, evidences in their lives.

On the back of the card, ask them to write an area in which they'd like to see more of God's presence in their lives. This could be in family relationships, compassion toward other people, understanding how His Word is true, or any other area of life.

Direct the students to trade cards with another person. Then stand in a circle and join in prayer, with each person in turn praying briefly for the person whose card they hold.

For more information on this kind of explanation and defense of the faith, see Evidence That Demands a Verdict by Josh McDowell (Here's Life Publishers).

21

Psalm 19:1–6

*The heavens declare the glory of God;
the skies proclaim the work of His hands.*

*Day after day they pour forth speech;
night after night they display knowledge.*

*There is no speech or language
where their voice is not heard.*

*Their voice goes out into all the earth,
their words to the ends of the world.*

*In the heavens He has pitched a tent
for the sun, which is like a bridegroom
coming forth from his pavilion,
like a champion rejoicing to run his course.*

*It rises at one end of the heavens
and makes its circuit to the other;
nothing is hidden from its heat.*

We know Him by ...

Romans 2:14–15

*Indeed, when Gentiles, who do not have
the law, do by nature things required by
the law, they are a law for themselves, even
though they do not have the law, since they
show that the requirements of the law are
written on their hearts, their consciences also
bearing witness, and their thoughts now accus-
ing, now even defending them.*

We know Him by ...

John 20:31

*But these are written that you may believe that Jesus
is the Christ, the Son of God,
and that by believing you may have life
in His name.*

We know Him by ...

Natural Knowledge of God

Revealed Knowledge of God

Read John 14:1–14.

Verses 1–4

Jesus is speaking just before He is to be crucified for the sins of the world. His disciples are worried because He has predicted that He would be leaving them. The verses that follow share His words of great comfort, assuring the disciples that God will still take care of them. His followers still don't quite get it. They want to know how God will do it, they want to see the heavenly Father.

Verses 5–6

What does Jesus point to as the "way, truth, and life"?

Verses 7–9

What is Jesus saying here? How do we know what God is like?

Just the Facts

1.
The gospels are trustworthy historical documents. They are accepted by scholars as primary source materials. It is generally accepted (even by secular scholars) that Matthew, Mark and Luke were written within 50 years of Jesus' death, and John within 65.

2.
In the gospels, Jesus tells us that He is God in human flesh (Matthew 11:27; John 10:30; 12:45).

3.
In all four gospels, Christ's bodily resurrection is described in great detail. Christ's resurrection proves His claim to deity.

4.
If Christ is God, whatever He says is true.

5.
Christ said that the Old Testament was true and reliable (Matthew 5:17–19). He also said that the New Testament would be infallible. (John 14:26; 16:12; 2 Peter 1:20–21)

6.
The Bible is God's Word, His revelation to all people about His nature and character. Through it He has provided the way to eternal life and shows us how to live in a real relationship with Him.

Our Three-in-One God

Ephesians 1:3–14

Study Outline

Activity	Time Suggested	Materials Needed
Opening Activities		
Begin with Prayer	3 minutes	
In the Box	10 minutes	An object concealed in a plain box
Studying the Word		
The Work of the Trinity	20 minutes	Copies of Resource Page 2; Bibles
The "Tri-Unity"	5 minutes	Newsprint or board, markers or chalk
Applying the Word		
How Does God Help Me?	10 minutes	Copies of Resource Page 2
Praying to the Trinity	7 minutes	

Opening Activities

Begin with Prayer

Holy God, the Father, the Son, and the Holy Spirit, You have created all things to be perfect; but our sin has destroyed perfection in your world. Forgive our sin for Jesus' sake and be present among us this day as we study Your Word. Give us the understanding of who You are so that we might grow closer to You. Open our hearts and minds as we study the three Persons of the Trinity. Help us to discover the unique work of each and recognize what You do for us in our lives. Bless our time together this day. In Jesus' name we pray. Amen.

In the Box

Choose an object that is unusual and unique and place it in a box. The object may be something like a a portable CD player or an old toy. Place the box near you and challenge the students to guess what it is by asking 20 or fewer questions. Choose an object that will challenge the students somewhat.

After 20 questions, if no one identifies the object, tell them what it is *but do not show the object to them.*

Say to the students: "When we study the triune God, we may feel like we are asking like 20 questions. We can't see Him fully, but we *can* know Him. The Bible gives us many glimpses of God as the Father, the Son, and the Holy Spirit. From all of these descriptions we can have a

Focus

Postmodern young people are keen on relationships. God makes Himself known to us and brings us into a relationship with Him through varying actions of three distinct "Persons" or natures. Each of these Persons has a unique identity (Creator, Redeemer, Sanctifier), but all are one God. God meets us, reveals Himself to us, and relates to us in His tri-unity. The one God who has created and redeemed us now calls us to see His presence in our lives.

Objectives

Through the power of God's Word, students will

1. Explore the mystery of the Three-in-One and the mystery of the one God who is unity in trinity and trinity in unity;
2. Recognize how each person of the triune God affects their lives through specific actions;
3. Rely on (and learn to pray to) God as Creator, Redeemer, and Sanctifier.

An Option

Leader, write GOD on the board. Ask the class, "Who is God?" Do not rescue them until they say it is the Father, Son, and Holy Spirit. Expect and allow the students to wrestle with this deceptively simple question, playing the role of someone who knows nothing about God.

After some time of struggle,

explain: "The Trinity is like the word GOD. All three letters together make up God. We attribute to each letter a specific job or task, but it takes all three to make up God. If you leave any part out, it's not God. No part is more important than the others. They are co-equal."

clear and accurate picture of God. You still haven't seen what is in this box, but you have a fairly accurate idea of what's in it. The same is true about the triune God. We don't fully see Him, but through God's Word we have a good idea of who He is.

Studying the Word

The Work of the Trinity

The Bible does not discuss each of the three members of the Godhead in detail, but it does help us get to know our triune God, to see glimpses into each of Them. That is why it is so important to look at all of Scripture. There is not a single, clear description of God that covers everything we know about Him. There are no passages which completely list all of God's work or the work of the three individual Persons. Since our picture of God must be based on the entire Bible, we must study it in its entirety, letting the clearest parts interpret those parts which are not clear. It takes the entire Book to see the picture that God paints for us of Himself.

There are a few passages, though, that speak of the whole Trinity. One such passage is Ephesians 1:3–14.

Direct the students to Ephesians 1:3–14. Although this passage does not cover everything about the triune God, it says enough for us to get a pretty clear indication of who God is and what He does for us. Read it aloud, or have volunteers read it aloud.

Distribute copies of Resource Page 2. Direct the students to work in pairs to list characteristics of the Father, Son, and Holy Spirit that Paul shares in the Bible passage. After allowing a few minutes for their work, invite different volunteers to share responses in each column. Responses could include

- Father—He blesses us with every spiritual blessing. He chose us. He creates the world. He adopts us as His children. He gives us grace and love.
- Son—He redeems us through His blood. He forgives our sins. He lavishes on us God's grace, wisdom, and understanding. He reveals to us the mystery of His will. He is the head of all things.
- Holy Spirit—He brings us God's Word of truth. He marks us—identifies us as God's possession—through Baptism. He guarantees our inheritance.

Summarize with words like these, reading the Bible verses necessary: "The Father's primary work is creation (Hebrews 11:3). To the Son, Jesus Christ, is attributed the work of our redemption (Acts 4:12). And the Holy Spirit has come for our sanctification, that is, for the whole work of bringing us to faith and leading us to live a godly life (1 Corinthians 6:11)."

The "Tri-Unity"

Say to the group, "We have looked at the differences of the three persons of the Trinity. We also need to examine what they share." On blank newsprint or on the board, write and discuss the questions that follow. Use the suggested responses in parentheses to assist and inform the discussion.

- What characteristics do the three Persons share? (Each one is fully God and is eternal—all three are from the beginning and will be forever. They share all knowledge, power, and presence. They are unchangeable and forever holy. They work to bring salvation to us and all people.)
- How do They work together? (The Trinity works in perfect cooperation. Each Person in the Godhead functions perfectly and and in union and conjunction with the Others.)
- What is Their goal? (The goal of the Godhead is to bring people to salvation. Each Person in the Trinity works toward the goal of redeeming people so that we might be with God in heaven. All things are centered around the principle that people must be saved from their sins.)

Applying the Word
How Does God Help Me?

Now that the work of God has been discussed, we are left with the question, "So What?" Young people need to know the facts about their God, but they must be able to apply that knowledge to themselves as well.

Direct the students again to Resource Page 2. Have them review the information about the work of the Trinity they have listed there. Ask them to identify ways in which each Person of the Trinity works in their lives. Prompt their thinking by asking them to consider things such as (1) basic needs, (2) relationships, (3) spiritual needs, and (4) prayer God has answered. Help them to discover for themselves that God is active and living in their lives each day. Stress that the most important action of God in people's lives is to bring them to—and sustain them in—a saving faith in Jesus.

Give the students three or four minutes to write responses. Then invite volunteers to explain how God is active in their lives.

Praying to the Trinity

Read aloud, or have volunteers read, Acts 4:23–31—Peter's prayer.

1. Ask a volunteer to summarize the prayer. (Peter spends a large portion of his prayer recalling with thanksgiving what God has done in the past, beginning with the creation. He then identifies his specific need and asks for God's help.)
2. What does Peter ask from God? (Peter does not ask to have the threats removed, but for strength to speak God's Word, heal the lame, and perform miraculous signs in Jesus' name.)
3. How does this contrast with how we tend to pray? (We may spend

An Option

If your group is large, you can have the young people form groups of four to discuss specific ways they know God is working in their lives. Sometimes youth do not want to speak in groups larger than four or five. This option allows those who are quiet to answer without as much personal risk.

An Option

Have the young people write down what God has done for them and then offer a prayer of thanksgiving.

little of our prayer time in thanksgiving—recalling what God has already done for us. We may also tend to focus our prayers on ourselves and our needs rather than praying for others.)

Point out that God already knows all of the things Peter recalled in his prayer. By recalling the things God has done for the whole world and for us, we can see how He is always actively involved in our lives. In so doing, the Holy Spirit reminds us where we would be without our great God. Keeping that perspective gives us a clear direction in our prayers for ourselves.

Challenge each student to list at least one thing that God has done for them, and the Person of the Godhead to whom that work is usually attributed. It can be anything from creating the world or giving us life today to specifics such as healing a parent or providing strength during temptation. When everyone has an answer, stand in a circle and start by having one person say what they chose to share about what God has done for him or her. Go around the entire circle, allowing everyone to contribute. Then close with a prayer of thanksgiving for those actions of God emphasizing the forgiveness, life, and salvation Jesus earned for us at Calvary. Invite petitions from the students on behalf of others.

The Work of the Trinity

The Father	The Son	The Holy Spirit

The Father works in my life by ...

Jesus works in my life by ...

The Spirit works in my life by ...

The Apostles' Creed, the First Article

I believe in God, the Father Almighty, Maker of heaven and earth.

In this first and shortest article of the Apostles' Creed, Christians summarize the basic beliefs about the first Person of the Trinity. They name Him "Father"—the Father of Jesus Christ and through Jesus, the spiritual Father of all Christians. And they name Him "Maker" or "Creator"—the One who existed before everything in space and time and the One who exceeds everything in power and might.

In the two studies that follow we look at this awesome God—the loving relationship He intended between Himself and His human creatures, the result of our sin upon that relationship, and the restoration He provided through His Son, Jesus Christ.

Our God Is an Awesome God

Job 38:1–11

3

Study Outline

Activity	Time Suggested	Materials Needed
Opening Activity (Choose one)		
Designer Stuff	5 minutes	A watch or other complex item
Will the Real God Please Rise?	10 minutes	
Studying the Word		
Absolute Power	15 minutes	Bible; paper and markers; poster board
Imagine This Discussion	20 minutes	Bible; Resource Page 3A
Applying the Word		
God's Light in Real Life	10 minutes	Copies of Resource Page 3B
Closing Activity		
In His Design	5 minutes	

Focus

We live in a world where many people no longer believe in an all-powerful God who creates and is relevant. Christians believe that God creates and sustains all things, including each of us! There is much confusion about who or what God is. For some, God's awesome qualities (divine attributes) cause fear. But for the Christian, God is a gracious, loving God who still takes care of us and will one day take us to our eternal home.

Objectives

Through the power of God's Word, students will

1. Explore the divine attributes of God;
2. See love as the essence of God and His relationship with us as His created beings.
3. Respond to God's greatness and love with fear, love, and trust.

To facilitate this activity, you may wish to write the 12 Bible references on index cards or slips of paper before class. Then you can distribute them quickly to the students.

Opening Activity

Designer Stuff

Use this activity or the one that follows, but not both.

Hold up a watch [or another complex item] and ask, "Where did this watch come from?" At first students may say the watch came from a store, warehouse, or factory. Be persistent. Lead the students to recognize that the watch was created by a designer who had great skill, knew how to use complex materials and tools, and carefully assembled hundreds of tiny parts following a unique plan. Only after it was built was it packaged and shipped to a store, where it was available for purchase and use. Ask, "Imagine all it took to get this watch working and into my hand. Do you think anyone would believe that this complicated thing just came together by accident?" Point out that the hand that holds the watch has millions of cells, arranged in complex systems to provide nutrition to each cell, allow mobility, provide strength, and allow coordination that cannot be matched by any machine. Say, "As amazing as some watches and other human inventions are, God's work is greater. He created the minds that create things like watches. Today's study will focus on the One who designed and created everything, our awesome God!"

Will the Real God Please Rise?

Use this activity or the previous one, but not both.

Ask your students, "What do you imagine God to be like?" Challenge the students to describe God as He is seen by themselves, their friends, and the world. People have different views of God. Some see Him as a sheriff, ready to bust people whenever they do wrong. Some see Him as a servant who is always ready to help people, especially those in desperate straits.

Some see Him as powerful but remote, like a self-absorbed professional athlete, who is out of touch with the realities of the world. Then say, "Today we're going to take a deeper look at who God is and how God continues to touch our lives and others' lives."

Studying the Word

Use both activities in this section.

Absolute Power

Provide blank sheets of paper and markers for the students. Assign the 12 verses that follow to 12 different students or groups. As the students read the Bible passages, they are to write the words in the passage that describe God, think of a symbol or simple picture that communicates that characteristic of God, and draw it on the paper. (For example, to represent God's eternal nature, one might draw a circle.)

After a few minutes, invite each student or group to share their symbol for the attributes in the 12 passages. As the students report, draw their symbol on a large sheet of paper or on the board, combining them to create a figure that represents God (a circle for a head, a lightning bolt for an arm, and so on). Here are the Bible references, attributes, and possible symbols:

1. John 4:24 (Spirit—a wavy outline)
2. Psalm 90:1-2 (Eternal—a circle)
3. James 1:17, Psalm 102:27 (Unchangeable—a rock or anvil)
4. Genesis 17:1, Matthew 19:26 (Omnipotent, all-powerful—a lightning bolt)
5. John 21:17 (All-knowing, omniscient—an eye)
6. Jeremiah 23:24 (Omnipresent, present everywhere—lines radiating out from a central point like a starburst)
7. Leviticus 19:2, Psalm 5:4-5 (Holy—a halo)
8. Psalm 118:1, 145:9 (Good—a happy face)
9. John 3:16, 1 John 4:8 (Love—a heart)
10. Deuteronomy 32:4 (Just—a gavel or the tables of the Law)
11. Titus 3:5, Exodus 34:6-7 (Forgiving, gracious—a cross)
12. 2 Timothy 2:13 (Faithful—a rising sun)

After hearing reports on all 12 passages, summarize by saying, "While we don't know yet exactly what God *looks* like—how He will appear when we see Him at the end of time—we do have a picture of what He *is* like. For one thing we know God loves and wants to save us and all people. He sent Jesus to earth to save us. As God brings us to faith

For Background Information

Celek, Tim, and Dieter Zande, The Soul of A New Generation. Grand Rapids: Zondervan, 1996.

McCoy, Michael C., A Christian Perspective on Creation vs. Evolution. St. Louis: Concordia, 1996.

Mueller, J. T., Christian Dogmatics. St. Louis: Concordia, 1934, 1955. See pp. 179–85.

He also leads us to a greater knowledge and understanding of who He is and what He is like. Let's see how this mighty God interacts with us, His creatures."

Imagine This Discussion

Ask the students to suggest the best professional basketball player (or athlete in another sport), the best musician, or a great person in another area of endeavor, focusing on someone who demonstrates the highest level of skill in that activity. Then ask what they would think if one of their peers criticized that famous individual in person. (For instance, suppose one of their peers suggested to Michael Jordan that he needed to improve his vertical leap, offensive maneuvers, and competitive spirit.) They will likely agree that we make ourselves look foolish when we think and act like we are better than others, when we are not.

Then ask, "Have you ever experienced a situation in which someone engaged in foolish criticism of another person?" Be prepared to share a personal example. Invite volunteers to share their stories.

Direct the students to Job 38:1–18. Distribute copies of Resource Page 3A. Divide the students into groups of three or four. Share the following background information with the students: "Job was a righteous man whom God allowed Satan to test with many trials. Job lost his wealth, health, and family (Job 1–2). In deep thought, despair, and frustration, Job eventually complains about God's injustice and asks that God explain His actions (Job 29–31)." Have the groups read God's reply and discuss God's eventual resolution of Job's situation, using the questions on the resource page.

After 10–12 minutes, gather the class and invite volunteers to share responses to the questions. Incorporate these points in the discussion of Job 38:1–18:

1. God is asking Job to consider himself in relation to God.

2. God's questions of Job in chapter 38 demonstrate that Job is *not* God's equal in any sense. Job cannot respond yes to any of them.

3. The gap between our abilities and God's is immeasurably greater. Comment that we too question God and wonder about Him when troubles and difficulties befall us.

Incorporate these points in the discussion of Job 42:10–17:

1. Thankfully, God responds to Job—and to us—with mercy, assuring Job of His love and care. He restores Job's former blessings and more!

2. Students will identify different attributes. Expecially affirm God's power and justice in chapter 38, and His love and faithfulness in chapter 42.

3. Over all His other characteristics, God is love. His justice and power are tempered by His great love for His people. That's good news for us. Though we are sinful people and deserve God's wrath, God in love provides the payment for our sins and the source of perfect submission in His Son, Jesus Christ.

For a More Extensive Study

Creation and evolution is a hot topic and continues to be debated in schools, homes, and churches. The teaching of evolution has led some to question the authority of Scripture and question the nature of God Himself. God's Word teaches a seven-day creation out of nothing (literally, "the earth was formless and empty," see Genesis 1:2). To explore the Bible's teaching in this ongoing discussion, study the following:

Read Genesis 1, Jeremiah 10:16, Romans 4:17, and Hebrews 1:2–3—God created the world out of nothing.

Read Matthew 19:4–6 and John 5:39—Jesus accepted the Old Testament as true and the Father as the Almighty Creator.

Read John 1:3; Colossians 1:16; and Romans 11:36—All things were created by God for His glory, not for the glory of people.

4. Allow volunteers to share their personal experiences of God's love, but do not force anyone to share. Be prepared to share an example of your own. Be sure to focus on how God has blessed you through Christ and His gifts of forgiveness, new life, and salvation.

Applying the Word
God's Light in Real Life

Say, "There's no doubt that we all know people—maybe family members or friends—who are hurting. Their hurt may be caused by divorce, broken relationships with friends, use and abuse of drugs and alcohol, or other problems. How can our relationship with an awesome Creator make a difference in those situations?"

Distribute copies of Resource Page 3B. Have volunteers read the two case studies. Discuss how God, in His love for us, might be at work in the two situations, bringing Christ's forgiveness and the life-changing strength and power of the Holy Spirit. Invite the students to suggest possible resolutions to each study.

Throughout the discussion help your students keep these points in mind:

• God is capable of helping us with any difficulty we face in this world.

• God works in our lives through His Word as it is read and spoken and lived by others. How can the Good News of Jesus help others through these difficult times?

• Those who seek assistance from sources other than God are depriving themselves of a tremendous source of help.

Ask, "What has this study taught you about God and your life?" Lead the students to see that God's love is not an abstract idea, but a real experience. In countless ways, including many that we cannot see, or of which we are unaware, God *is* at work in our lives.

Closing Activity
In His Design

In groups, have each person design a prayer that (1) thanks God for who He is and for entering their lives through Jesus and (2) asks Him to enable them to share His awesome love with others. For example, "Lord, thank You for being the awesome, all powerful God You are. No one is an accident, Lord. I pray that You be with my younger brother who is suffering from asthma. Be with him and watch over him. In Jesus' name I pray. Amen." Invite volunteers to share their prayers as the closing prayer.

Imagine This Discussion

Read Job 38:1-18. Then discuss these questions:

1. What is God asking Job to do in these verses?

2. Can Job respond to God's questions? Why or Why not?

3. How might we apply God's words to Job to our own lives? How are Job's comments similar to the criticisms we might see in our lives.

Read Job 42:10-17. Discuss these questions:

1. How does God eventually respond to Job?

2. Which of the characteristics from Resource Page 2A is God showing to Job?

3. What does Job's story tell us about our relationship with God?

4. Think of a time that God loved you and touched you in a special way.

Solid Truth

God's Light in Real Life

Rebecca is an average student at your high school who doesn't have a lot of friends. She's hoping to become more popular, but her parents don't have the money to buy her designer clothes or pay for the activities that her friends do. She's hoping to become more popular by becoming 'looser' in her morality. Maybe if she has sex and can enjoy partying more, others would like her better. She can dress looser, drop some of her studying habits, and quit attending youth group and church.

Tom has been angry for some time. His parents recently went through a divorce. Tom lives with his mother, who is very angry with his father. Tom sometimes gets blamed by his parents for things he doesn't do. With all the stress in his life, Tom's grades have dropped off, and he gets punished at home for that, too. Tom has been showing his frustration at school by talking back to teachers, getting into fights, and breaking long-term friendships—including his friendship with you. You fear that he might do something foolish.

Discuss

- Is God capable of helping people through their problems?

- How can God help others through these difficult times?

- What things do people turn to besides God in time of trouble?

- What has this study taught you about God and your life?

- What hope and power do we have because of Christ's death and resurrection.

Our Disfigured Image

Romans 7:14–25

4

Study Outline

Activity	Time Suggested	Materials Needed
Opening Activity		
The Reality of Sin	10 minutes	Several pieces of 2 × 4 (wood) scraps, distressed; fine sandpaper
Studying the Word		
The Battle Within	15 minutes	Bibles
Applying the Word		
The Battlefield	15 minutes	Copies of Resource Page 4; pencils or pens
New Wood	10 minutes	An unmarred piece of 2 × 4
Closing		
The Weight of Sin	5 minutes	1 or 2 heavy books for each student

Opening Activity

The Reality Of Sin

Before class, take a 2 × 4 and cut it into pieces that are about a foot long. Use a hammer to pound the wood, make nail holes, smear dirt on its surface, and drip paint or wood stain on it.

Divide the class into groups of three or four. Give each group a beat-up piece of wood and some fine sandpaper. You may also wish to provide markers, stickers, colored tape, and the like. Tell the groups that their job is to make this wood as beautiful as possible. They are to try to cover up or get rid off the scars. Allow the groups about five minutes to work.

When they have finished "dressing up" their wood, they are to make a brief (one- or two-minute) sales presentation to the class, as if trying to sell their piece of wood. When each group has made its presentation, ask, "How is this wood like sin in the world? How do we try to hide sin or change its appearance? What are some sinful things we try to make look as though they are okay for us?"

Allow time for responses (answers will vary according to the experiences and maturity of your group). Then point out that sin for us is a reality. It is part of our lives. We try to cover it. We try to get rid of it. We try to call it something else or make excuses for it. We try to make it hip. The truth is that we are all sinners. We all fall short of God's Law. Sin is a struggle for all of us, just as it was for the apostle Paul.

Focus

"Nobody's perfect!" That simple and often-stated truth reveals a tremendous problem for all who by God's grace acknowledge Him and seek to be in relationship with Him. Though we were created in His image, that image has been lost because of sin. On our own we are not the people He created us to be. But God did not leave us "on our own." In His love, He recreates and sustains us spiritually through the sacrifice of His Son.

Objectives

Through the power of God's Word, students will

1. affirm the basic truth that "no one is perfect," all have sinned;
2. identify the reality and result of sin in their own lives and the lives of those around them;
3. give thanks for God's action to overcome our sin through His Son.

Advance Preparation

Well before class locate a length of 2 × 4 lumber. Cut it into several foot-long sections—one section for every 3–4 students you expect in class and one extra. "Distress" all but one of the pieces of wood as described in the activity. If you use paint or stain to mar the wood, allow sufficient time for drying so that students do not get paint on their clothes.

If your class is large, pair up

groups to make their presentation and sales pitch to each
other. Allow just a minute or
two for each side to present
its pitch—about four minutes
total.

Studying the Word
The Battle Within

Start by asking the question: "In what way is your 'spirit willing,' but your 'flesh weak'?" Possibilities include starting an exercise program, getting all homework done on time, having a regular devotion time, always being nice to parents, and many others.

Ask the students to turn to Romans 7:14-25. Introduce the study by saying, "There is a battle in all of us. It is a battle with sin. Today we are going to see the reality of sin in Paul's life—and in ours. Paul tells us how the Law helps us know what sin is. Paul struggles with sin. He knows what he's not supposed to do, but because of his sinful nature he does it anyway."

Read, or have volunteers read, the Romans passage. Then discuss it using the following questions.

- What does Paul share about his own attempts to follow the Law? (Verses 15, 19—Paul laments that he is unable to follow the Law—to do the good the Law demands and avoid the evil it forbids.)

- What does Paul say about the Law? Himself? (Verse 14—The Law is "spiritual," one of God's tools; Paul is "unspiritual … a slave to sin," subject to sin's persistent rebellion.)

- What did Paul blame for his continuing failure to do good? (Verses 17-20—Paul clearly points to his sinful nature, the sin we all inherit since the fall of Adam and Eve.)

- How do you relate to Paul's struggle? (All Christians this side of the grave continue this struggle with sin. The "old Adam" [our sinful nature] and the "new Adam" [Christ living in us] are at war until our final victory and rest.)

- How does Paul describe his struggle to do what is right? (Verses 21-23—He uses the analogy of warfare and battle.)

- Is Paul's experience of moral failure only his struggle or is it universal? (Scripture testifies that "all are sinful" [Romans 3:23, 5:12]. Sin is a universal experience of people.)

- Why do you think God's Law was given to us to follow: (1) A means to follow in order to be saved? (2) A guide to follow once we are saved by grace? (3) A tool for self-reflection that shows us our sinfulness? Support your answer from the passage. (All three points are valid. The Law teaches us that we are sinners in need of a Savior. But salvation *does* come through the Law. The problem for us is that no one can keep the Law perfectly since sin entered the world. Jesus earned our salvation by keeping God's Law perfectly. Now, by God's grace through the work of the Holy Spirit, we desire to keep God's Law.)

- Paul turns to Christ in verse 25. How did Jesus rescue us from the curse of sin? (For our sinful things we do, Christ lived a life of "passive obedience." He suffered and died so that we might receive forgiveness of sins and be called God's forgiven people. For the good things we fail to do, Jesus also lived a life of "active obedience." He fulfilled the Law so that we might receive God's gift of Christ's right-eousness and be called saints of God.)

Applying the Word

The Battlefield

Distribute copies of Resource Page 4. Read Romans 7:13 to the class: "Did that which is good, then, become death to me? By no means! But in order that sin might be recognized as sin, it produced death in me through what was good, so that through the commandment sin might become utterly sinful." Invite the students to pretend that they are pilots on their own personal battlefield, depicted on the resource page. On the battlefield are buildings that represent temptations. The missiles represent God's actions on our behalf and the spiritual fruit that His Spirit produces in our lives. Their mission is to target the temptations we struggle with and bomb them with God's power, given to us through His Word, so those temptations may be overcome by God at work in our actions and attitudes by the power of His Word. Point out that these missiles aren't empowered by man-made explosives, but by the Holy Spirit living in us through faith. (Samples of temptations include gossiping, cheating, stealing, cursing, lying, drinking, using drugs, laziness, denying God, not respecting parents, or not witnessing. Examples of the Spirit-led attitudes and actions include reading the Word, showing godliness, kindness, honesty, purity, selflessness, dili-gence, character, faithfulness, integrity, and respect.

In each building they should write a brief summary of a struggle. They can write the name of the missile over the building or on the missile itself and draw a line from the missile to the building, doing this for as many struggles as they can think of or have time for. Encourage hon-esty and assure them that the page will not be shared with anyone else.

It is important to point out that out temptation can only be overcome by the power of the Holy Spirit working through God's Word and Sacraments. Only through His power can we be kind, selfless, encour-aging, and the like.

New Wood

After a period of time bring the group back together again. Say, "We all have areas of our lives where we struggle. We want the godly character-istics, but often our sinful desires take over. What are some real-life examples of that happening?" Encourage the students to share experi-ences that demonstrate the struggle of wanting to do what is right yet having sin take over.

After a period of sharing, bring out a piece of good wood and lay it on the ground next to the beaten-up pieces. Read aloud Romans 7:24 to the class. Then say, "Paul wanted to be like this clean, new piece of wood, but often felt he looked like the others. We also experience this struggle. The reality is that sin often controls us more than we want. We can cover it up. We can't say it's not our fault. We can't wipe it away. What is our answer? [Read 7:25a.] The answer is Jesus. Jesus paid the price for our sin. He sees how disfigured we are because of sin. He gave His life for us so that we are no longer slaves to sin. We can overcome sin in our lives through Jesus and the power of the Holy Spirit living in us."

Closing

The Weight of Sin

Have the students hold out their least dominant arm with the palm facing up. Place a large book or two on their palm. Say, "The struggle and weight of sin can be a burden, and it can be painful. There is a solution to our problem."

Read 1 John 1:8-9: "If we claim to be without sin, we deceive ourselves and the truth is not in us. If we confess our sins, He is faithful and just and will forgive us our sins and purify us from all unrighteousness." Then invite the students to bow their heads and imagine that what they hold in their open hand is the sins they need to confess to God.

As you read the following prayer, encourage the students to reflect on their sins each time you pause. Then pray this prayer:

"Most merciful God, we confess that we are by nature sinful and unclean. We have sinned against You in thought (pause for students to confess thoughts that were sinful), word (pause again), and deed, by what we have done (pause) and by what we have left undone (pause). We have not loved You with our whole heart (pause); we have not loved our neighbors as ourselves (pause). We justly deserve Your present and eternal punishment. For the sake of Your Son, Jesus Christ, have mercy on us. Forgive us, renew us, and lead us, so that we may delight in Your will and walk in Your ways to the glory of Your holy name. Amen."

(*Lutheran Worship*, p. 158, © 1982 Concordia Publishing House)

Walk around the classroom and remove the books from the hands of the students. As you are doing this read, or have a student read, Romans 8:1-2: "Therefore, there is now no condemnation for those who are in Christ Jesus, because through Christ Jesus the law of the Spirit of life set me free from the Law of sin and death."

The pray, "Father, we know that there is a battle within us. We have been disfigured by sin. Help us, by the power of Your Spirit, to follow Your Law. When we fail, Lord, point us to Your grace. Thank You for Jesus, the forgiveness He provides, and ability to begin anew He earned for us by keeping the Law perfectly in our place. Empower us by Your Spirit to live our lives serving You as we rejoice in the the gift of our salvation. In Jesus' name we pray. Amen."

On the Way Out

Give the students suckers or Tootsie Pops. Instruct them that they are to enjoy the candy on the way home, but they are not allowed to chew it. The temptation will be to chew the candy after a while, but urge them to hold out. Let the sweetness of the candy serve as a reminder of the sweet forgiveness Jesus freely offers us, having kept God's Law perfectly on our behalf.

Solid Truth

The Apostles' Creed
the Second Article

[I believe] in Jesus Christ, His only Son, our Lord, who was conceived by the Holy Spirit, born of the Virgin Mary, suffered under Pontius Pilate, was crucified, died and was buried. He descended into hell. The third day He rose again from the dead. He ascended into heaven and sits at the right hand of God, the Father Almighty. From thence He will come to judge the living and the dead.

The Creed's second article confesses Jesus to be the Christ—the Anointed One of God—and details in concise sentences His life and ongoing purpose. It is a confession, not a complete doctrinal statement. It does not say everything about Jesus, but it covers the basics.

The studies that follow treat Jesus Christ—His incarnation, His unique identity, and His resurrection and ascension. While they explore Scripture texts that go well beyond the simple language of the Creed, these lessons also do not say everything there is to say about our Lord and Savior. As we come to know Him, we begin a life of relationship and discovery that is completely fulfilled only when we will live with Him in eternity.

In the Flesh

Hebrews 2:5–18

5

Study Outline

Activity	Time Suggested	Materials Needed
Opening Activity (choose one in addition to prayer)		
Prayer	5 minutes	
That Small?	10 minutes	An infant's or toddler's clothing
Qualified?	10 minutes	
Studying the Word		
Job Application: Savior	20 minutes	Bibles; copies of Resource Pages 5A and 5B
Applying the Word		
Jesus in Me	15 minutes	Index cards
Closing Activity		
Prayer	5 minutes	Bibles

Opening Activity

Begin with a prayer like this one: "Lord Jesus Christ, we begin in Your holy name. You created us. You know us well. In spite of our sinfulness, You still love us. You lived, died, and rose again for us. Allow us to know You better as our best Friend and as our Savior. Amen."

That Small?

Use this activity or the next one but not both, unless you have extra time.

Show the students the clothes or shoes of an infant or toddler, something that would be much too small for them now. Ask them to guess how old a child might be who would wear those clothes. Invite them to remember and share things they remember or have heard about their lives at that age (fears, embarrassing moments, things learned, likes/dislikes).

Point out that, even though they have grown too big to wear a toddler's clothes or shoes, they can remember and understand what it is like to be a little child. God's Word tells us that God Himself became a real human being. He grew, learned, worked, slept, ate, felt emotion, and died. God truly understands us because He has "been there, done that." And by becoming a human being, Jesus was the perfect Substitute for us to receive the punishment for our sin. This lesson intends to show why this is true and what it means for us.

Focus

"I just wish someone could understand." Jesus does! Though He is God eternal with the Father and the Spirit, Jesus set aside His divine power to join us in space and time (the state of humiliation). He was born like us, lived like us, and died like us (but did not sin like us). No matter what our problems, temptations, and needs, we have a God who has "been there, done that."

Objectives

Through the power of God's Word, students will

1. discuss the two natures of Christ and tell why the Savior had to be both true God and true man;

2. identify the importance of the incarnation for Jesus' work of redemption and for His compassionate concern for people;

3. rejoice in and turn to the One who knows them and their needs "best of all."

You may wish to dress the part of a surgeon in this activity, bring in some medical equipment and tools—stethoscope, medical forms, and the like. Attempt to convince the students that you are qualified to do the job, arguing that the clothes or the other props are evidence of your ability.

If your class is larger than six students, assign this discussion of job applications and Resource Pages 5A and 5B to small groups of 3–4 students. Allow about 12 minutes for the small group discussion and spend another 5 minutes or so reviewing the resource pages with the whole group.

Qualified?

Use this activity or the previous one but not both.

Ask the students if any of them would be willing to let you perform open-heart surgery on them. You might share with them a few details about the heart (it has four chambers, is located in the chest area, and pumps blood) and assure them of your willingness to "read up" on things beforehand. (If you *really are* a heart surgeon, choose another specialized field such as auto mechanics.) Ask the students to list the qualifications you, or any of them, would need in order to become a surgeon (a medical degree, board certification, hospital privileges, experience, equipment, and recommendations from other people). Write the students' responses on the board or on a sheet of newsprint.

Point out that Jesus Christ met two very necessary qualifications to be our Savior from sin. Jesus was both true God and true man. This study will reveal what this means for us.

Studying the Word
Job Application: Savior

Ask students to share any experiences they have had applying for or interviewing for a job. Focus on the common aspects of such an activity—did they fill out job applications, experience an interview, dress in a special way for an interview, take any tests, or have special training?

Distribute copies of Resource Pages 5A and 5B, an incomplete job application for the position of "Savior of the World." Review each section of the application, working with the students to complete it. Specific activities, discussion questions, and suggested responses are listed under the various subheadings.

Requirements

Read or have a volunteer read the requirements. Encourage students to think about what difference it would have made if Jesus were only human, or only divine. This topic is discussed later in the application.

Background Information

Review and complete the background information. (Place of birth—Bethlehem; Citizenship—Israel, although one could make the case for putting "heaven" in this blank; Ethnic origin—"Jewish" on His mother's side and "divine" on His Father's; Mother's name—Mary; Father's name and occupation—add Joseph, a carpenter. Help the students see that Joseph and God were both fathers to Jesus, though Joseph's relationship with Jesus was not a biological one.)

Education and Experience

Read, or have a volunteer read, the things listed here. Ask the students what importance these things had in Jesus' task of saving the world from sin. (Jesus frequently used the Old Testament Scriptures to explain truths about God and who He was. Jesus, being true God, was well acquainted with humankind. He is the Creator and had interacted with human beings since the beginning. He knew the problems and pain that sin had brought into their lives. He had great love for people.)

Description

Remind the students that the Scriptures provide us with *revealed knowledge* of what God is like. The Bible is very clear about both the human and divine natures of Christ.

Assign each of the Bible passages under "Human Characteristics" to a student or pair of students. Have them write the human characteristics found in their verses. After about three minutes invite students to share their responses. (Suggested responses: Matthew 4:2—was hungry; Matthew 26:38—felt sorrow; Matthew 27:26, 46, and 50—suffered and died; Mark 4:38—slept; Luke 2—was born; Luke 4:1-2—was tempted and hungry; Luke 24:39—was made of flesh and bones; John 2:13-16—felt anger; John 11:35—cried; John 19:28—got thirsty.)

Then look at the divine characteristics. Ask students what *evidence* is available to support these divine characteristics. (Miracles and healing—the Scriptures record many miracles, from the changing of water into wine to the post-Resurrection catch of fish; prophesies—the people could see for themselves that the prophets' words were fulfilled in Christ's actions [see Matthew 11:5]; all-knowing—many considered Jesus to be wise beyond the ability of any human being, a few people encountered Jesus' miraculous knowledge, including the woman at the well [see John 4]; forgives sins—no one except God can see the heart, but many saw the joy in the lives of forgiven people; worthy of honor—again not a visible quality, but a result of the sum of Jesus' actions; sent by God—revealed to many by Jesus' other actions; sinless—the centurion at the crucifixion declared Jesus to be a "righteous [sinless] man" as did many of the apostles.)

Look again at "Necessary Requirements" at the beginning of the application. Help the students match a few of the divine and human characteristics to aspects of these requirements.

Ask the students what difference would it have made if Jesus were only a divine being or only a human. Christ had to be true man so He could take our place under the Law and keep it in our place, and so He could suffer and die in our place for our failures to keep the Law. He was tempted just as we are, but without sin. He can help us when we are suffering or tempted in any way. Christ also had to be true God so that His fulfillment of the Law and His life, suffering, and death would be a full payment for the sins of all people. And He had to be true God so He could defeat Satan and death for us.

References

Writers of the New Testament, in a sense, are references for Jesus, that we may know and believe that He truly accomplished salvation for us

If you have time, challenge the students to find examples of each of these characteristics in the Bible using concordances or other Bible-reference guides.

(John 20:30–31). Direct individuals or small groups to (1) look up the passages in this section, (2) write down the words that testify to Jesus' humanity and divinity, and (3) report to the class. The responses should be as follows (italics have been added):

- John 1:1, 10—"In the beginning was the Word, and the Word was with God, and the Word *was God. … the world was made through Him.*" [divinity]

- John 1:14—"The Word *became flesh* and made His dwelling among us. *We have seen His glory, the glory of the One and Only,* who came from the Father, full of grace and truth." [humanity; divinity]

- Romans 5:19—"Through the *obedience of the one man* the many will be made righteous." [humanity]

- Galatians 4:4–5—"God sent *His Son, born of a woman,* born under law, to redeem those under law, that we might receive the full rights of sons." [divinity and humanity]

For Office Use Only

Finally, direct students to read this section silently. Point out that the writer to the Hebrews comments on the significance of what God's only Son, Jesus, did for us by becoming a true human being. These comments confirm that Jesus meets the requirements for being the Savior of the world. Have the students underline the phrases that speak of Jesus sharing our experiences. (Hebrews 2:9—"He might taste death for everyone"; Hebrews 2:14—"shared in their humanity"; Hebrews 2:18—"He himself suffered when He was tempted, He is able to help those who are being tempted.") Conclude by saying, "Through His incarnation as the God-Man, Jesus lived and died so that you and I could live a new and eternal life, die to sin, and be raised from death as He was. Only in Him do we have hope."

Applying the Word
Jesus in Me

Ask, "How does Jesus' humanity, His temptation to all kinds of sin, give you comfort or encouragement?" (He struggled with temptation and suffered God's punishment in our place, He knows what it's like to be sad or discouraged.) Then ask, "How does His divinity, His ability to resist sin, give you comfort and encouragement? (For example: He could overcome sin and death, He can do something about my problems even when I can't, He can forgive me.)

Tell the students that, because Jesus became true man, He understands the struggles, temptations, and needs we have. Because of His love for us, we can in turn show His love and understanding to others. Distribute index cards and pencils. Have students think of someone in their life that needs love and acceptance. (For example: a younger sibling, a friend who is having problems, or a parent who is frequently tired). Instruct them to write that person's name on the card, with a brief description of that person's needs. On the other side of the card, students should write one or more ways they can reflect Christ's love to that person. (For example, they might write "I will spend some time playing with my younger brother," or "I'll invite my friend over and listen patiently as she talks.") Encourage students to take the card with them and post it in a place that will remind them to follow through.

Conclude by saying, "The blessings that Jesus came to bring are ours through faith. By faith, now we can be a blessing to others."

Closing Activity

Discuss the question, "Why are you glad to know that Jesus became a human being like you?" Then have students look up Colossians 1:21-22 and read it together. Close with a brief prayer of thanks to Jesus, who has made us holy through His holy life, death, and resurrection.

As part of this activity, you could have everyone stand in a circle. Allow each person to stand in the middle of the circle while the rest of the class reads Colossians 1:22, substituting the person's name each time the word you is read. (For example: "But now He has reconciled Tom by Christ's physical body through death to present Tom holy in His sight, without blemish and free from accusation.")

A Prayer of Praise

Write a prayer of praise. Have students look at Hebrews 2:5–18. Pick out phrases to complete the statement, "I praise you, Lord, for …" (Example: Using verse 14— I praise you, Lord, for destroying the power of death and the devil.) You may want to have them write their phrases on a sheet of newsprint to put on display or on a small slip of paper to aid them in sharing.

JOB APPLICATION

Position   *Savior of the World*

Requirements

It is necessary that the Savior be **true man** because

- only a true man could act in our place under the Law and fulfill it for us;
- only as true man could Christ suffer and die for our guilt, our failure to keep God's Law perfectly.

It is necessary that the Savior be **true God** because

- only as true God was His fulfilling of the Law, His life, suffering, and death, a sufficient ransom for all people;
- only as true God could He overcome death and the devil for all people.

Background Information Please complete the following:

Applicant: *Jesus*

Birth date: *3 B.C. (Human)*   *From Eternity (Divine)*

Place of birth:

Address: *Unknown location in Nazareth*   Citizenship (country):

Ethnic origin:

Mother's name:

Mother's occupation: *Homemaker*

Father's name: *God Almighty*

Fathers' occupation: *Creator; One true God*

Education and Experience List only the most recent or most important information.

Education: *Well acquainted with all of Scripture*

Past experience: *Has created and sustained all creation from eternity; demonstrated unconditional love, justice and power throughout history*

Description (Human Characteristics:)

Matthew 4:2— _____

Matthew 26:38— _____

Matthew 27:26, 46, 50— _____

Mark 4:38— _____

JOB APPLICATION, continued

Description (Human Characteristics:), continued

Luke 2— _____

Luke 4:1-2— _____

Luke 24:39— _____

John 2:13-16— _____

John 11:35— _____

John 19:28— _____

Description Divine Characteristics:

Performed miracles　　　　*Fulfilled prophecies of the prophets*

All-knowing　　　　　　　*Forgave sin*

Was sent by God　　　　　*Is worthy of honor and glory*

Was sinless　　　　　　　*Was able to rise from death*

References Write the words that prove Jesus the Savior to be true God and true man.

Name:

John:　　John 1:1, 10 _____

_____

John 1:14 _____

_____

Paul:　　Romans 5:19 _____

_____

Galatians 4:4-5 _____

_____

For Office Use Only Underline phrases that represent *experiences Jesus shared* with humanity.

Hebrews 2:9　But we see Jesus, who was made a little lower than the angels, now crowned with glory and honor because He suffered death, so that by the grace of God He might taste death for everyone.

Hebrews 2:14　Since the children have flesh and blood, He too shared in their humanity so that by His death he might destroy him who holds the power of death—that is, the devil.

Hebrews 2:18　Because He Himself suffered when He was tempted, He is able to help those who are being tempted.

Solid Truth

The Way, Truth and Life

Acts 4:8–12

Study Outline

Activity	Time Suggested	Materials Needed
Opening Activity (Choose one)		
True and False	15 minutes	
The Law of the Land	15 minutes	Copies of Resource Page 6A; pencils, pens, or markers
Studying the Word		
One Name, One Way, One Truth, One Life	20 minutes	Bibles; copies of Resource Page 6B
Applying the Word (Choose one or more)		
The Key to Life	10 minutes	A key for each student; fine-tip, permanent markers
Your Favorite Color	10 minutes	
Closing Prayer	5 minutes	

Opening Activity

True and False

Use this activity or the next one, but not both, unless you have extra time.

Assemble the students in the middle of the room. Designate the left side of the room for truth and the right side for falsehood. After the students hear each of the following statements, they are to move to the side that represents their opinion about its truth.

• Mickey Mouse has three fingers on each hand. (False. He has four.)

• The *tilapia macrocephala* fish carries its fertilized eggs in its mouth and doesn't eat until the little ones are born. (True.)

• Each year, the canary sings a new repertoire of songs to attract female birds, never singing the old songs again. (True.)

• The male crab "shakes hands" with the female with whom he chooses to mate. (True.)

• The mudskipper fish can climb trees. (True.)

Discuss the following questions:

1. How important is it to know what is true? When does it matter most?

2. Is truth relative? Are some things true at some times but not at others?

Limit this activity to 15 minutes. You will not settle these questions yet. Just get the students thinking and talking.

Focus

In a postmodern society that boasts of religious tolerance and open-mindedness, Christians face a multitude of religious options. God's Word testifies that only those who have faith in Jesus Christ as their Redeemer share eternal life with God. This truth, though it runs counter to the popular culture, will have eternal significance for young people and their friends.

Objectives

Through the power of God's Word, students will

1. see that Christianity is unique among religions in dismissing works as a means of pleasing God;

2. give thanks for the redemption that is theirs through faith in Jesus Christ;

3. express concern for others they may know who do not yet rely on Jesus Christ as the only "way and truth, and life."

The Law of the Land

Use this activity or the previous one, but not both, unless you have extra time.

Distribute copies of Resource Page 6A and divide the class into groups of three or four students. On the resource page are two stone "tablets" that students will identify with the tables of the Law from Exodus 20. However, these tablets are blank. Challenge each group to come up with their laws for society. After 8-10 minutes, give each group a chance to share their "laws" and tell why they should be followed. Limit each group to two minutes. After each group has had the chance to share, ask the following questions.

If your class is small, use just one group. Discuss the purpose of each "law" as it is written. Then go directly to the discussion questions. *If your class has more than 12 students*, have two groups share and explain their "laws" to each other. Then discuss the questions with the class as a whole.

1. What would life be like without laws? (Chaotic, scary; you'd live in fear, etc.)

2. How do laws come into being? (Most laws are made by various levels of human government. They are frequently based on God's Law. Some personal customs or habits ("laws" in a loose sense) may be based on one's feelings. God's Law, of course, was given to us directly by Him. Moses and other inspired writers recorded it in the Bible. God's Law is also written on our hearts, our consciences.)

3. Does obeying the society's laws or keeping God's Law determine who will go to heaven? How would you respond? (As you discuss, share these important points: [1] Theoretically, someone who kept the Law perfectly could earn eternal life. However no one except Jesus ever has or ever will be perfect. [2] If the standard by which people are judged were less than the perfection God required, as some religions teach, one could never be certain of where one stood—"Have I done enough or been good enough?" [3] Because Jesus was true God as well as true man, He was able to keep God's Law perfectly in our place. Therefore the only "road" to heaven must be through Him. Jesus says it clearly, "I am the way and the truth and the life" [John 14:6].)

Studying the Word
One Name, One Way, One Truth, One Life

Distribute copies of Resource Page 6B. Create groups of three or four students. Assign each group one or more of the Bible references from the resource page. Allow about eight minutes for the groups to read their passages and discuss the questions. Then invite each group to report their results to the class. As each group reports, make sure they include the following information:

Acts 4:8–12

1. Peter spoke by the power of the Holy Spirit (verse 8).

2. The "rulers and elders" to whom Peter is speaking were the same basic group who plotted to reject Jesus—that is, have Him arrested and crucified. They feared Jesus' teachings, including His claims to have come from God (verse 11).

3. The people to whom he spoke relied upon their own ability to obey the Law. They believed they were righteous before God on their own merit.

John 14:5–6

1. Jesus had just told the disciples He would be leaving soon and had predicted Peter's denial. Thomas was troubled and confused, unable to understand the deeper meaning in Jesus' words.

2. Thomas would have known that he was at least "headed in the right direction" as a disciple, a follower, of Jesus.

3. Jesus' words here show the exclusive character of the Christian faith, in that there is only one way to heaven—through faith in Jesus Christ. Nonetheless, God loves and desires the salvation of all people as the next passage will show.

1 Timothy 2:3–6

1. God desires that all people come to faith in Jesus and be saved from eternal condemnation for sin.

2. The truth is explained in the next two verses—Jesus is the Mediator and Sacrifice for all people.

3. Jesus is the Mediator (an advocate) for all people. Help students understand what this means for us—He prays for us before God's throne of grace.

4. Again, Jesus died for all people. He did this out God's great love for all so that forgiveness and new life would be available to all.

Proverbs 14:12

1. Many people claim the right to "make it on their own." The Bible is clear that "on our own" won't make it; when it comes to eternal life, we need a Savior, Jesus Christ.

2. Answers will vary. Our culture urges that we be *tolerant* of the views of others and *inclusive.* It is not "politically correct" to be exclusive in anything, including religion.

3. In spite of the world's views, God's Word is clear. It *does* make a difference what people believe and to whom they look for salvation. "Tolerance" in spiritual matters can cost a person *eternal* life!

4. Open this question up to all your students. Challenge them to identify one or more people, but don't require them to name names.

Applying the Word
The Key to Life

Give each person a key. As they hold the key, review these questions with the students: (1) What does the world say is the key to a relationship with God? (2) What does the Bible say is the key? After allowing volunteers to respond, remind the students that Jesus said that He is the Way, the Truth, and the Life and that no one comes to the Father

Keys can be purchased inexpensively at most hardware or discount stores. Their miscut keys may be available for free.

If you have a large class, divide into groups of 5–6 students.

except though Him. Paul reiterated that point, saying that salvation is found in no other name but Jesus. Pass around fine-tip, permanent markers. (Watercolor markers won't work.) On one side of the key have the students write "John 14:6" and other the other side write "IKTT" ("I know the truth"). Have them put the key on their key chains with their house or car keys as a reminder that Jesus is the key to eternal life, and that this truth needs to be shared!

Your Favorite Color

Allow a volunteer to name his or her favorite color. Then instruct the rest of the group to convince this person that he or she is wrong, that another color is better. The students can argue, provide incentives, or do anything within reason to change this person's mind. Encourage the students to persevere beyond their initial attempts, trying new means of persuasion.

After five minutes, discuss the experience.

- How does having a definite favorite color make it easier to resist the claims of others? (It may lessen the temptation to switch.)

- How does knowing what is true and right make living in this world easier? (Answers will vary. Point out that having a standard against which to measure things makes decisions more clear-cut.)

- Is the truth that Jesus is the only way to heaven an opinion (like having a favorite color) or is it something else? What? (It's a fact; the Bible makes it clear that salvation comes in no other way—Acts 4:12.)

- Does knowing the truth that Jesus is the only way to heaven make life easier or harder? (Students could argue either way: easier, because they don't get tempted to believe other things; harder, because everyone can seem to be against that truth.)

- Since we know that Jesus is the only way to heaven, how does that change the way we see other people? (Other people desperately need to hear that truth; it's like having a sure cure for a disease that kills 100 percent of its victims! How can we keep it to ourselves?)

Closing Prayer

As the students hold their keys in their hands, close with this prayer:

"Father, we thank You for Your incredible love. You provided a way for us to live with You now and forever. We can't earn it by our good works; You give it freely. Thanks for revealing that truth in Jesus Christ. Give us power by Your Holy Spirit to witness to this truth. We want our friends, our school, our parents, and the whole world to have eternal life through Jesus Christ. In His name we pray. Amen."

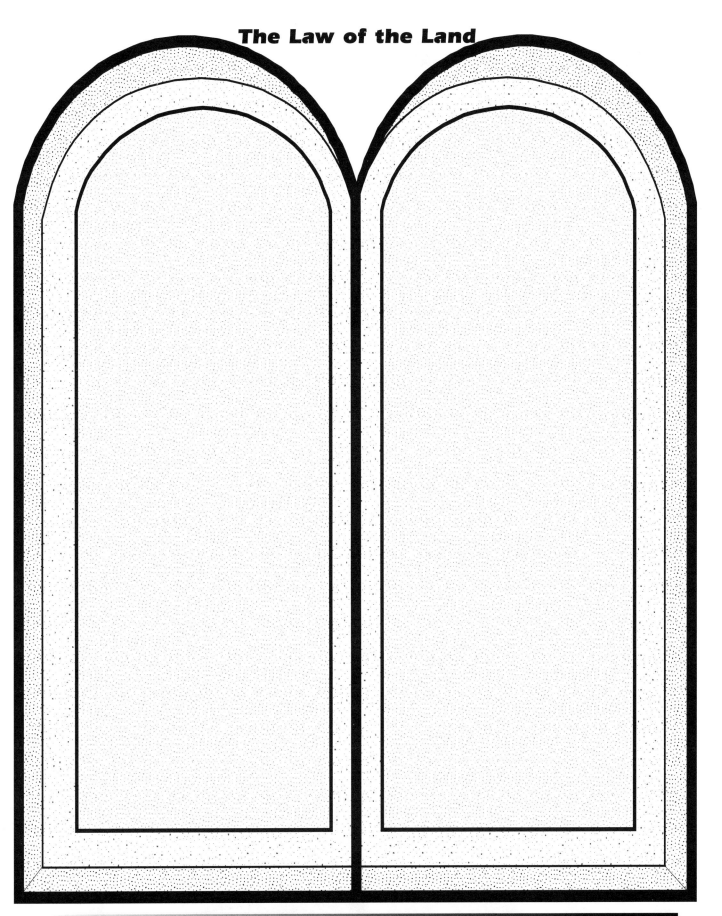

Solid Truth

ONE Name Way Truth Life

Read Acts 4:8–12.

1. What empowered Peter to speak? (verse 8)

2. How was Jesus the "stone" rejected by the "builders"? Why? (verse 11)

3. Why was Peter's statement in verse 12 such a challenge to his audience?

Read John 14:1–6

1. Why did Thomas ask his question of Jesus? (verse 5)

2. Do you think Jesus's answer helped Thomas? (verse 6)

3. In what way is faith in Jesus Christ exclusive or narrow?

Read 1 Timothy 2:3–6

1. What does God want? (2:4)

2. What is the truth? (2:5)

3. For whom is Jesus Christ a mediator? (2:5)

4. For whom did Jesus give Himself? Why? (2:6)

Read Proverbs 14:12

1. How does this verse tie in with what people in the world today believe?

2. Why do you think people have a hard time believing that Jesus is the only way to heaven?

3. Why is it important to tell people about the truth of Jesus Christ?

4. Whom do you need to tell? Who needs to know that Jesus is *the* way to enjoy a relationship with God?

Raised to Rule

1 Corinthians 15, especially 15:12–22

Study Outline

Activity	Time Suggested	Materials Needed
Opening Activity		
Begin with Prayer	3 minutes	
Alternative Advertising	10 minutes	Paper and pens or pencils
Studying the Word		
What You See Is What You Get	10 minutes	Bible reference books (optional)
If/Then	15 minutes	Bibles
Applying the Word (Choose one)		
Risen and Ascended Lord	10 minutes	
More than Once Around?	10 minutes	
Closing		
God Is Our All in All	10 minutes	

Opening Activity

Begin with Prayer

Dear Jesus, thanks for all You have done for us—Your life of obedience, Your suffering and death, Your resurrection, and Your ascension. Through You we have the forgiveness of sins and life eternal. Help us remember that You are all-powerful and rule the whole universe. Yet You are with us at all times, knowing our needs and caring for us completely. Be with us as we study Your Word. Amen.

Alternative Advertising

Briefly discuss advertising techniques with your students—how advertisers try to convince you that you need their product. Ask which advertisements students believe are truthful and which ones they find misleading. What would it be like if all advertisements were completely truthful?

Have the students create examples of *very* honest advertisements. (For example, "Use our mouthwash; it'll make your stinky breath tolerable—for a few minutes anyway." Or, "Buy our packaged lunch; your kids will toss less of it in the trash than the ones you make.") Then have the students think up truthful advertisements which are positive, but lack phony hype. (For example, "Use our mouthwash; it won't guarantee you'll get the girl, but it will take that awful taste out of your mouth." Or, "Buy our packaged lunch; it's tasty, it's easy, and you'll know your kids will have eaten something good today.")

Focus

Jesus' resurrection is the assurance of forgiveness of our sins, the affirmation of absolution. Our debt is fully paid. For lives trashed by sin, the resurrection is restoration, a recycling of broken lives to fullness through Christ's work. His state of humiliation is ended. Christ, still fully human and fully divine, now ascends into heaven, and is able to be present and to rule everywhere.

Objectives

Through the power of God's Word, students will

1. see in Christ's resurrection and ascension the affirmation of their forgiveness and proof of Christ's divine power and authority over sin, death, and the power of Satan;
2. identify the personal benefits of a risen Savior;
3. rejoice in the forgiveness of sins and presence of Jesus Christ in their daily lives.

An *Active* Option

If you have a large group, have small groups act out their advertisements. Award a prize for the most painfully true advertisement.

Conclude by pointing out that we all would prefer advertising that helped us get our "money's worth." We like to get what we expected when we buy something. This is the issue that Paul deals with in this study. Is the resurrection of the body a reality, or are Christians guilty of false advertising?

Studying the Word

Use both activities if you have time. Otherwise, skip to "If/Then."

What You See Is What You Get

Review the background for the Bible text you will study—
1 Corinthians 15:12–22. If you have time, expand on the brief background information provided here, using Bible reference books available locally. Among the important details to share with the students are these:

• The apostle Paul was writing from Ephesus, another city that had a new Christian church.

• Corinth was a cosmopolitan port with a very diverse population and many religions. Paul was writing to instruct the Corinthian church to repent of the wrong things they were doing (sexual immorality, divisions and factions in the church, misuse of the Lord's Supper) and, in faith, hold fast to the Gospel.

• At the heart of this section is Paul's argument against some members of the Corinthian church who misunderstood the resurrection and its importance. His "if/then" argument in verses 12–19 leads the readers to his central point, "But Christ has *indeed* been raised from the dead."

If/Then

Have students read 1 Corinthians 15:12–13. Ask a volunteer to restate the problem Paul is addressing. (Some people were denying the possibility of the resurrection of the body from death. If there is no resurrection, then not even Christ has been raised, and neither will we be raised.)

To help the students understand Paul's logic and the importance of what he is saying here, have them create negative if/then statements about things in life, nature, etc. (For example, *if* there were no clouds, *then* there could be no rain. Or, *if* there were no work, *then* we would not appreciate rest.)

Now have the students find the *if* and *then* statements Paul makes in verses 14–19. As they read the verses silently, create the following chart on the board or on newsprint.

Students may ask questions beyond the scope of the information presented. If you have a number of beginning Bible students or others with little background in Scripture, consider spending some time before this activity to review one of the accounts of Jesus' resurrection in Matthew 27–28, Mark 14–15, Luke 23–24, or John 19–20.

v. 14—If _____ [then] _____

and _____

v. 15   More than that _____

v. 16—If _____ then _____

v. 17—If _____ [then] _____

[and] _____

v. 18—   [and] then _____

v. 19—If _____ [then] _____

Have the students help you fill in the chart as you work through the verses. Your finished chart will look like this one:

v. 14—If <u>Christ has not been raised</u> [then] <u>the Apostles' preaching is useless</u>

and <u>so is our faith</u>

v. 15   More than that <u>those who believe in the resurrection and testify to it are false witnesses</u>

v. 16—If <u>the dead are not raised either</u> then <u>Christ has not been raised</u>

v. 17—If <u>if Christ has not been raised</u> [then] <u>our faith is futile</u>

[and] <u>we are still "in our sins" (that is, guilty of sin)</u>

v. 18—   [and] then <u>those who have died in Christ are lost</u>

v. 19—If <u>our faith only gives hope for this life</u> [then] <u>we are to be pitied more us than anyone</u>

Point out that Paul goes to a lot of trouble to make his point here. Ask, "Why?" (The resurrection of Christ is central to our faith; our eternal destiny hinges on this truth.) This line of logic leads to Paul's main point in this section: "But Christ *has indeed* been raised from the dead" (verse 20).

Have the students create positive *if/then* statements and compare them to verses 21-23. (For example, *if* it rains, *then* the ground will be wet; *if* you throw an object up in the air, *then* it will come back down.) Paul uses this *if/then* logic to show the absolute reality of Christ's resurrection. There are consequences to any action; in this case the consequence of Christ's resurrection for those who believe in Him is our own resurrection. This fact is the ultimate "truth in advertising"—what we see (Christ's resurrection) is what we get (our own resurrection on the Last Day).

This truth can be expressed like a mathematical formula:

Perfect world <+> sin <=> death

Before the Fall, in the perfect world God created, humans would have lived forever. When Adam's sin entered the equation all human beings died.

Death <+> Christ <=> eternal life

In the broken world, humans are doomed to death and separation from God. Adding Christ's sinless life, His sacrificial death and His resurrection to the equation results in life—eternal life, resurrected life.

Applying the Word

Unless you have extra time, choose one of the following activities, but not both.

Risen and Ascended Lord

Have the students look up Matthew 1:22–23. Focus on the name by which the child (Jesus) is to be called: *Immanuel.* Focus on the meaning of this name, "God with us." Jesus *is* God, and He *is* man, *with us, one of us.*

Review with the students the blessings of the human nature of Christ (see study 5). Briefly stated, Christ in His incarnate state was able to experience everything that we experience—hunger, sorrow, pain, loneliness, exhaustion, temptation, and even death. He is able to understand our needs in a personal way and can fill them in His grace. In His role as our "great high priest" (Hebrews 4:14–16), He is able to sympathize with our every human need. We can therefore call upon Him in every circumstance, confident of His mercy and grace.

Remind the students that these blessings continue even as Jesus Christ "sits at the right hand of God the Father," reigning in heaven. Provide blank paper and pencils or pens. Invite the students to write specific concerns they may have for themselves or others in the form of sentence prayers. Plan to incorporate these prayers into the closing.

More than Once Around?

Perhaps the most common contemporary contradiction of the Christian resurrection of the body lies in the idea, found in many Eastern religions, of rebirth or reincarnation. Originating in early Hindu scriptures, rebirth theories are central to many other Eastern religions, including the various types of Buddhism. Reincarnation is also a belief of followers of the New Age.

Because this is so, many young people today will have early exposure to the concepts of *karma, reincarnation,* and *Nirvana.* Resource Page 7 offers a brief comparison of the basic concepts of rebirth that are common today and the basic teachings of the Bible. Distribute copies of the resource page to the students and review it one section at a time.

A more detailed study of the subject of reincarnation will be found in the study on eastern religions in One God, Many Gods, © 1998 CPH, stock number 20-2427, available from your local Christian bookseller in the fall of 1998 or by calling CPH at 1-800-325-3040.

For more detailed information about reincarnation and its roots in Hinduism consult The Hindu Connection: Roots of the New Age, by A. R. Victor Raj, © 1995 CPH, stock number 12-3256, or a dictionary or encyclopedia of religion.

Closing

God Is Our All in All

Remind the students that, since it is true that Jesus continues to share His human nature after the resurrection and ascension, He is fully in touch with all kinds of human needs. He continues to care about our day-to-day cares, joys, and worries. He also cares about our eternal destination. He longs for us to experience His resurrection in our own and be with Him eternally. Have the students share (1) any hurts or hopes they are experiencing in their day-to-day lives, (2) ways in which they have seen Christ present in their hopes and joys, and (3) ways in which they can focus on His care in dealing with their hurts and worries.

Close with prayer, allowing time for the students to pray for themselves or for each other (using the sentence prayers they have written in the "Risen and Ascended Lord" activity, if you used it). When the students have spoken their petitions, close with a prayer thanking God for the gift of His Son, our *risen, ruling* Savior.

More than Once Around?

Reincarnation

1. Reincarnation is the belief that the human soul passes through a succession of lives (the transmigration of souls). In early Hindu scriptures, these lives might be not only human but plant and animal as well. Western versions of reincarnation usually limit rebirth to human lives. This transfer of soul is immediate—at the moment of death, the soul is reborn in a life already prepared for it.

2. Reincarnation is closely related to the eastern Law of *Karma*—the belief that the good and evil done in past lives are the cause for our circumstances and personal characteristics in this life, and that our actions and attitudes in this life will determine what our future life will be.

3. The goal of reincarnation is to have an upward cycle of existence, each life lived on a higher plane than the previous one. This is achieved through self-discipline and denial. "Salvation" (the Hindu concept is *Nirvana*) is attained when all desire is purged and the soul at death is completely free from human existence. This emphasis often results in a pessimistic view of life, for each new birth is in reality a penalty for not having been good enough in past lives.

4. Originating with Hinduism, this belief is also found in the many forms of Buddhism. Religions and organizations more common in the Western world that share Hindu roots and rebirth emphases include Transcendental Meditation, Hare Krishna, Eckankar (the science of soul travel), the Church of Scientology, and the New Age movement. All are essentially "monistic," in that they believe that man and God—indeed all things—share the same substance and can ultimately be united.

Christ/Resurrection

1. The Bible is clear that all humans have only one life after which comes death, judgment, and eternity either with God or apart from His presence forever (Hebrews 9:27). Each birth is a new creation by God, a new soul, and each death a permanent departure from this world and doorway to eternity. Only Jesus, who is truly God, had existence before His birth on earth (John 1:1).

2. Scripture teaches that the one life of each ungodly person is controlled by sin, and that the one life of each believer in Jesus Christ is controlled by the Holy Spirit (Romans 7:5–6). The sins of the ungodly do indeed condemn them in "next life"—that is, eternity (Romans 1:20, 32). The sins of those who believe in Jesus are forgiven and washed clean (Colossians 1:13–14). The good works of the ungodly and believers alike gain them no merit before God nor affect their place in eternity.

3. While reincarnation relies on the self for progress toward salvation, Christianity teaches the grace of God who provides the atonement for and forgiveness of our sins by Jesus Christ through His perfect life, once-for-all sacrifice on the cross, and resurrection from the dead (1 John 4:10). For those who by faith become God's people, life is not ultimately a time of suffering but a time of joy (Romans 15:13).

4. In contrast, the Christian faith gives identity and purpose for those who are God's people (Ephesians 2:10). We acknowledge our role as His creatures and look to our Creator and Redeemer for His blessings now and in the life to come.

The Apostles' Creed, the Third Article

I believe in the Holy Spirit, the holy Christian church, the communion of saints, the forgiveness of sins, the resurrection of the body, and the life everlasting. Amen.

The final article of the Apostles' Creed encompasses the great variety of work attributed to the Holy Spirit, who works in and through God's people. Through the Gospel, the Word and Sacraments, the Spirit creates faith in Jesus as Savior and Lord. He calls Christians together in Christ's body, the church, and provides the gifts that support the body. He makes the faithful holy and stirs us to the good works that reflect His presence in us. He keeps us in faith in this life and into eternity.

These then are the studies in this final section of *Solid Truth*. May the Spirit work through them in the lives of those who study God's Word.

Peace with God a Free Gift

Romans 3:10–31; 5:1–2, 9–11

Study Outline

Activity	Time Suggested	Materials Needed
Opening Activity (Choose one)		
What Do You Need?	10 minutes	
Extra Credit	5 minutes	A credit card
Studying the Word		
Christ's Free Gift	20 minutes	Bibles; a mirror
Applying the Word		
Peace Received and Shared	20 minutes	Copies of Resource Pages 8A and 8B
Closing		
A Verse to Remember	5 minutes	Index cards and rulers (optional)

Opening Activity

Pray this prayer to begin your study:

"Heavenly Father, Giver of every good and perfect gift, bless us with Your presence and strengthen us as we study Your Word. Strengthen us always with the gifts of Your Spirit, especially the gift of peace. We pray this in the strong name of Jesus who is our Lord and Savior. Amen."

Choose one of the following activities, but not both.

What Do You Need?

Ask students to turn to Galatians 5:22–23. As they are looking up the passage, write the nine gifts of the Spirit mentioned in these verses on the board or on newsprint (love, joy, peace, patience, kindness, goodness, faithfulness, gentleness, and self-control). Ask a student to read aloud the passage.

Invite volunteers to share the gifts of the Spirit (Galatians 5:22–23) they would like more of and why. Whether or not volunteers mention the gift of peace, conclude this activity by saying, "In the 60s a popular song went, 'What the world needs now is love, sweet love.' Today our world certainly seems to be experiencing a severe shortage of *peace*. People are searching for peace in life, using various means to search for that peace. What means might people use to try to find such peace?" (Answers of course will vary; examples abound—money, fame, achievement, etc.) "Why will these not bring us the peace we need?" (Because they do not have the power to present us blameless and pure before God. When we die the power of these things, what little they actually have, also dies.) "In this study we will learn more about Christ's free gift of peace with God and how that gift affects our lives."

Focus

Postmodern teens receive early and extensive education in hype: image is everything and everything is image. Such market-savvy young people may strongly resist or warmly embrace the free gift of faith by which God leads us to trust in Jesus Christ as our Savior of sin. Though our redemption is a free gift to us from a loving Father, it was not easily obtained but purchased at great cost through perfect life (passive obedience) and the suffering and death (active obedience) of the only Son of God. He lived a life we could not live and died as only He could die, to pay a debt we could not pay.

Objectives

Through the power of God's Word, students will

1. recognize that we cannot earn peace with God, forgiveness for sins, and new life in Christ—these things are the free gifts of God through faith in Jesus;

2. weigh the cost of the salvation Jesus purchased for us on the cross;

3. rejoice that faith is a free gift, given by God through His Word.

Encourage your students to memorize the gifts of the Spirit. For a helpful memory device, remember this: the first three gifts of the Spirit (love, joy, peace) are each

65

one syllable; the second three gifts (patience, kindness, goodness) are each two syllables; and the third three gifts (faithfulness, gentleness, and self-control) are each three syllables.

Extra Credit

Ask if any student has a credit card that she or he can show to the class. (If not, be prepared to show one of yours.) Ask this person to display the card and to describe how a credit card works. Explain that some stores take only certain credit cards. Some places even advertise with a certain amount of pride that they take a particular card. If you try to make a purchase at a certain store, you might find out that you can't, because your credit card is no good there.

This study explores the teaching of justification by faith. This is the biblical teaching that God, for the sake of Christ, declares us not guilty, in spite of our sinfulness, solely on account of the death of Christ on the cross. By His death and resurrection we have all the *credit* in God's sight that we need. It's called justification by faith, or the forgiveness of sins.

Studying the Word
Christ's Free Gift

Display a small, handheld mirror. Remind the class of the words of the wicked queen in the story of Snow White, "Mirror, mirror, on the wall, who's the fairest of them all?" She was enraged to find out that it was not herself, but Snow White, who was the fairest one. Look in the mirror and make a positive statement about yourself, such as "When I look in this mirror I see ..." an honest businessman or a capable mother of three. Pass the mirror to a number of volunteers and encourage them to share what they "see" in the mirror (talented singer, good driver, employee of the month, community volunteer, active church member).

Point out that we are all aware of our own image. We want it to be the best it can be. And we'll do things to improve it. But what does God see as He looks at us?

Invite students to turn to Romans 3:10–31 and read the passage to themselves, taking particular note of verses 20–24. Then discuss the following questions.

Verses 10–18: All Have Sinned

1. How would you summarize this section of Paul's letter to the Romans? (Not one of us has an image before God other than that of unrighteous sinner).

2. Note or underline all the negative images in these verses. They paint a pretty ugly picture of our sinful condition. Are things really that bad? How can sin be so universal among people? (Sin was the topic of Study 4. Briefly stated we are dealing with at least three areas of sin—the bad things we do, the good things we fail to do, and the inherited [though not genetic] sinful condition that plagues all humans since Adam and Eve [see Romans 5:12 and following]. Sin is not just a matter of what we do or don't do, but of who we are.)

3. Do you think most people see that this is a problem? Why or why not? (Opinions will vary; use the question to discuss the larger issue.

Yes, sin certainly is a problem, although a lot of people don't seem to know or care. Even some Christians aren't very clear at times that their sins have the potential to eternally separate them from God. Note that one way this passage describes the sinner's—that is, *our*—condition is not knowing the way of peace [verse 17].)

Verses 19–22: Under the Law or in Christ?

1. This section of Romans divides people into two categories—those who are under the Law and those who have faith in Jesus Christ. Who are those "under the law" and what is their fate? (Everyone at one time was included in this group [verse 19]. It still includes those who would rely on the Law, and their ability to keep it, as a means of pleasing God, gaining favor with Him, and inheriting eternal life. Since no one can obey the Law sufficiently, this approach is doomed to failure.)

2. What is the alternative to striving for righteousness [being right or good] under the Law? (Verses 21–22 remind us that faith in Jesus Christ is the only alternative. We are either covered by His righteousness or our sins are fully exposed to God's sight.)

Verses 23–28: Peace with God through Faith

1. Define the terms *justified, redemption,* and *atonement.* (Justified—justified margins are made even; justified people are declared right with God; His justice has been satisfied. Redemption—the process of buying something or, in this case, *someone* back; ransomed; rescued. Atonement—the act of paying what is owed; making payment to someone for a debt or injury. All three terms are pictures of what Christ does for us, to deal with our sin.)

2. What is the significance of the little word *freely* in verse 24? Doesn't everything have a price? (The sinners don't justify themselves; the hostages don't rescue themselves; the debtors cannot repay on their own. God does it—freely, without cost to us, but not without cost. He paid the price of the suffering and death of His only Son to rescue us from sin.)

3. Does that mean we are no longer sinners? (No, but we stand before God as *forgiven* sinners. We haven't quit sinning, but God, for the sake of Christ, chooses to accept us as His people, freely, gracefully, undeservedly, without reservation.)

4. Read Romans 5:1–2, 9–11. The positive images here contrast with the negative ones in chapter 3:10–18. Where can the world find peace and joy? (In reconciliation, a renewed friendship, with God through faith in Christ. That faith is a gift from God through His Word and Sacraments. We'll study more about that in future studies.)

Applying the Word
Peace Received and Shared

Ask a student to look up John 14:27 (Jesus promises peace to His followers) and read it to the class. Ask another student to find and read

An "A-Cross-tic"

(Optional Activity)

An acrostic is a phrase in which the first letters of each word spell another word. G-R-A-C-E can be an acrostic for "God's riches at Christ's expense." Invite the students to work in groups of two or three to develop an acrostic definition of P-E-A-C-E. (If students find this exercise impossible to complete, you can remind them that this is an indication of how elusive peace can be at times, even in the lives of Christians.)

John 20:19–21 (Jesus, in His resurrection, brings peace and sends His disciples out to share it with others.)

Ask volunteers to share, on the basis of these passages and others, what makes peace possible in a believer's life? (The presence of Jesus, His death and resurrection—He showed them His wounds and the disciples were overjoyed, our peace comes with a price, the price of the life of God's Son).

Point out that only Jesus can bring true peace to a person's life. But even true peace is hard to experience because of our sin. In a believer's life, just as there is a mixture of saint and sinner, grace and sin, so there is also a mix of spiritual anxiety and peace. Perfect peace will be ours, however, for eternity in heaven.

Remind the students that Jesus sent His disciples out to share His peace. That is His challenge for us as well.

Distribute Resource Pages 8A and 8B. Read and discuss as many of the case studies there as you have time for. Invite students to take the roles in each script. Allow them to be creative and to ad lib as they wish. Discuss each case study using the questions on the resource page. Answers to those questions will vary according to the thoughts and situations of your students. Challenge students to find the way of peace and forgiveness in each study. Throughout the discussion, also challenge the students to test the responses for reality with questions such as the following:

1. Would this work in real life?
2. Will it bring real peace to the situation?

Closing

A Verse to Remember

Write the following verse on the board, on newsprint, or on index cards for each student: "Let the peace of Christ rule in your hearts, since as members of one body you were called to peace" (Colossians 3:15). Purchase some inexpensive, wooden rulers, one for each student, or have the students create rulers out of stiff cardboard. Remind the students that since we have peace with God, the free gift of forgiveness, we can also be ruled by peace in our daily lives. God has forgiven us all our sins for the sake of Christ. We can not measure up to God's demands on our own. But God does forgive us. Have them write the verse on the back of the ruler and take it home as a remembrance of this important truth.

The conclude with this prayer:

"Gracious God, we confess our sinfulness to You. We know that we cannot stand before You and offer You anything that can bring us Your peace and acceptance. Instead, we acknowledge that You have purchased us from all sins by the death of Your Son, Jesus. This alone brings us the forgiveness and peace that we need. Thank You, Father, for this wonderful gift of salvation and peace. Help us, by Your Holy Spirit, always live in this forgiveness and peace. Let us experience the joy that they bring to our lives. We pray this in Jesus' name. Amen."

1. The Case of the Perplexed Parishioner

The phone rings in the pastor's office. Pastor Garaway answers.

Pastor Garaway: Hello.

Ted: Hello, Pastor. This is Ted Liederkranz.

Pastor: Hi, Ted. What's up?

Ted: I'm perplexed about all the angry words I heard at the church meeting yesterday.

Pastor: Ted, I know what you mean. Some of the issues at these meetings sure do get people worked up, don't they?

Ted: Well, I was part of that, too, and now I want you to know that I don't feel so good about it.

Pastor: Hindsight is always 20/20, isn't it? Ted, I appreciate your call. And I want to assure you of God's forgiveness for any angry words you may have spoken.

Ted: Thanks, Pastor. Now, is there anything I can do to help the situation?

Pastor: Actually, Ted, there is. I could use your help in not only addressing the issue that was being discussed, but also in dealing with *how* it was discussed. Interested?

Ted: Sure. Just say the word.

Pastor: OK, here's what we'll do …

For discussion: *Pastor and Ted have embarked on a specific peace mission. What would you advise them to do or say?*

2. The Case of the Petulant Parent

Dad confronts daughter Sarah in the family room. Sarah is sitting on the floor watching TV.

Dad: Sarah, how many times do I have to remind you that washing the dishes is *your* responsibility. Everyone has chores to do in this house, and I expect you to follow through on yours. I'm tired of looking at dirty dishes every time I walk through the kitchen.

Sarah: I'll get to them in a few minutes, Dad.

Dad: Too late. I've already done them. And you're grounded. No company, no social engagements, and no telephone calls this weekend.

Sarah: Dad! You can't do that! I'll die of boredom! And I *was* going to wash the dishes. You just got there before I did.

Dad: Sorry, Sarah. Somehow I've got to get through to you about this.

Sarah: You just don't understand.

Dad: Apparently, you don't either.

(Dad stomps down the hall. Sarah is left to wonder how her bike-less weekend will go. "Why is he always on my case?" she wonders to herself.)

For discussion: *What can Dad and Sarah do to resolve their anger toward one another?*

3. The Case of the Caustic Chem Lab

Two students are working together in chemistry lab. One of them spills the contents of a test tube on the lab table.

Dan: Now look what you made me do!

Matt: What?

Dan: You bumped my arm and now we have this stuff all over everywhere—including our lab notes. We have to do all our work over.

Matt: I didn't even touch you.

Dan: Well, this stuff didn't spill all by itself.

Matt: Maybe you just want to blame somebody for your clumsiness.

Dan: And maybe you're afraid to take responsibility for something you did.

Matt: Man, you're something else!

(The teacher arrives on the scene.)

Mr. Naclau: What seems to be the problem here, fellas?

Dan and Matt (pointing at each other): Ask him!

For discussion: *How can Matt, Dan, and their teacher, Mr. Naclau, work through this situation?*

4. The Case of the Crabby Customer

Jennifer is working in a fast-food restaurant. A customer walks up to the counter.

Jennifer: May I help you?

Customer: I want a burger, fries, and a cola.

Jennifer: I'll get that for you right away. It'll be $3.73.

(Some time passes.)

Customer: Isn't my order ready yet?

Jennifer: Let me check. *(She leaves and comes back.)* It'll be right out.

Customer: It's about time. I thought this was supposed to be a *fast* food restaurant.

Jennifer: I'm sorry, Sir. We're having some problems today. Some of our employees on this shift didn't come in.

Customer: I've got problems of my own. And I'm in a hurry.

Jennifer: Let me check again.

Customer: Let me talk to your manager while you're at it.

Jennifer: I'll go get her. *(She leaves and returns with the manager.)*

Manager: What can I do to help you, sir?

Customer: I'm still waiting for my food, and this clerk here has been very rude and unhelpful.

Jennifer: What?

For discussion: *What can Jennifer and her manager do to resolve this situation peacefully?*

One Body

1 Corinthians 12, especially 12:12–20; Ephesians 4:1–16

Study Outline

Activity	Time Suggested	Materials Needed
Opening Activity		
Prayer	3 minutes	
Structure Building	15 minutes	Craft materials
Studying the Word		
How Things Work	15 minutes	Bibles; blank paper and pens or pencils
Working Together	15 minutes	Copies of Resource Page 9; Bibles
Applying the Word		
What about You?	10 minutes	
Closing Prayer	3 minutes	

Opening Activity

Prayer

Open with a prayer like this one:

"God—Father, Son, and Holy Spirit—bless our time together. Unite us as a group of Christians who are present to study Your Word and learn from the Holy Spirit all You have to teach. Show us how we can be many different members but part of the same body of Christ. Show us our part in the body of Christ and help us contribute to the work of Your church. We ask it in Jesus' name. Amen."

Structure Building

Gather craft items such as like cardboard, yarn, glue, tape, craft sticks, cardboard tubes, and pipe cleaners. Divide your group into small groups of four or five people. Mix strong leaders, mature young people, and quiet introverts in each group. Give each group the task of working together to create something with the supplies. They can create a building, cross, symbol, tower, or anything that comes to mind. The groups will have 10 minutes to plan and build their structure. Give them two important instructions:

• Each group should choose a leader. It will be that person's responsibility to make sure everyone has a task to do that contributes to the project.

• The leader will direct the efforts of the team. The leader's decisions will be final and binding on all group members.

Focus

Postmodern young people desire relationships and thrive on interdependence. For them the concept of the body of Christ will be good news, especially as God enables them to experience it through the work of the Holy Spirit.

Objectives

Through the power of God's Word students will

1. recognize the interdependence of Christians in the body of Christ;

2. grow in their ability, by God's grace to see their place in the body and fulfill it;

3. give thanks for the one Spirit at work in them through faith.

This lesson plan assumes a class size of eight students or more and specifies some small-group activity. If your class has fewer students than eight students, you can easily omit the small-group structure, do the activities in one "small group," and skip the instructions to share work or make reports to the whole class. In such a case some activities will take less time.

When the groups finish, gather them together again and have each group explain what they made. Discuss the following questions:

1. How did you decide who would be the leader?
2. How did you feel about the team's work and your contribution to the project? How important were you to the project?
3. Were the assignments and contributions of each team member equal? Should they have been? (Answers will vary according to the students' feelings. Affirm each student's role in the project. Even those who sit back and admire can be helpful.)

Point out that, even in the church, everyone has a role and each one's part is important to achieving the goal. We may not always value our role or feel valued, but God's plans involve each of us.

Studying the Word
How Things Work

Direct students to again work in the teams established for the opening activity. Have the students locate 1 Corinthians 12:12–20 in their Bibles. Challenge each of the small groups to write their own version of the text using an analogy that is different from Paul's description of how body parts work together. (Possibilities include a baseball team, an assembly line, a family, a car, or anything with parts that work together.)

Allow about 10 minutes for the group work. Then invite each team to share their version of the text. Encourage them to point out ways that their analogy supports the concept that God revealed through Paul to the Corinthians and to us. Then process the activity with these questions:

- What are the benefits when an *interdependent* group—one whose members need to work together—functions correctly? (The group's goals can be reached more quickly, fully, and enjoyably.)
- What happens when members of such a group cannot or will not do their work? (The group may fail, it may function poorly, or other group members may have to work harder. In rare cases, there may be no observable result.)
- What does that tell us about the church, which Paul describes as an interdependent body? (God's plan is for a fully functioning body, but sin may prevent that from happening.)

Working Together

Distribute copies of Resource Page 9. Read, or have a volunteer read, Ephesians 4:1–16. Have the students work in pairs or small groups to discuss the questions found on the page. After about 10 minutes, invite volunteers from each group to respond to the questions. Use the following notes to clarify and expand on the students' answers.

1. Paul is writing from a prison in Rome, where he awaits his trial. He also sees himself as being bound up in Christ and eternally connected to Him. Thus, he calls himself a prisoner of Jesus Christ.

An Option

If time allows, the groups may act out their version of the text. This could become a game of charades. The group may act out their particular example, and the rest of the groups may guess what it is. If there is only one small group, you may still have them act out their example. It will help them to work together to solve problems and to work toward a goal.

Roles Others Fill

You may wish to take time to help young people identify the many people who work in your congregation. Many do not know how much effort goes into a typical Sunday. Have the young people list those they saw serving in various ways just today identifying the roles and counting the total number of people—the pastor, organist and musicians, ushers, elders, women's guild, acolytes, greeters, teachers, custodians, and others.

2. The word *calling* may be better translated as *vocation,* which depicts a lifetime of service. Verses 2–3 describe the answer vividly—our vocation is to include humility, gentleness, patience with each other, love, and community peace. The first four build the last one. Help your students make a real-life connection here by asking them to think about the ways they can serve God now, using these four God-given characteristics. Remind them that their true worth comes from Jesus Christ, who gives them the power to live out this vocation—and forgives them when they do not.

3. Keeping "the unity of the Spirit" means living in peace and harmony with those in your Christian community. This happens when we take ourselves out of the center of things, let others share the limelight, and put God's work first. As we learn to serve God with our talents without taking credit, we contribute to the community and thus live in peace.

4. Help the students evaluate themselves. Do not rescue them, but let them wrestle with how they are doing with each other. Remember, teenagers are often self-absorbed as they are learning to become independent adults. They rebel against parents and authority. This is part of the natural process of human development, but it is not an excuse for misbehavior among Christians. The community concept is crucial, yet nearly impossible for them on their own. Forgiveness must be emphasized so that they can continue to mature without being condemned.

5. Ideally, each person should answer this and let the other members of the group agree or disagree. This is a great chance to grow as a group and individuals. If this seems too risky, just have individuals describe how they feel about themselves without group response.

6. It means that Christ has given us a share in His body and that we receive the gifts that we need. In Jesus Christ and His church, none of us should feel unimportant or useless. Christ Himself has given us talents and jobs to serve Him. No job is greater than the next. The whole body works together. We have the power to do that through the gifts Christ has given us.

7. Verse 12 says "to prepare God's people for works of service." Ask, "How do we as a church prepare you for works of service? Could we do a better job? How?" Accept all answers and pass good ideas on to the congregation's leaders.

8. They are tossed back and forth. People will follow any kind of teaching that comes along. Ask, "Why is it important for our whole church body to accept the same doctrine (teachings)? How does doctrine serve the body of Christ?" By being united in doctrine, we are anchored to Christ and nothing can move us. Then we are not easily deceived, but are given the power to tell the truth in love. Grounded in Christ, we have real answers and solutions and are less subject to doubt. Christ holds us all together as we serve Him in our Christian communities, because He is the Head to whom we all belong.

Applying the Word
What about You?

Redirect the students to Resource Page 9. Remind them of the "How Things Work" activity. Each person plays an important part in Christ's body, the church. Sometimes people fill more than one role. The chart on the bottom of the resource page lists four subgroups in the body of Christ: (1) the congregation, (2) the youth ministry, (3) the family, and (4) a group of friends.

Have the students work again in small groups to identify up to six functions, or roles, they think are important in that subgroup and who does that task or fills that role. Encourage them to use their personal subgroups (their congregation, their family, their group of friends) *and* to include themselves in the chart—what role(s) or function(s) do they fill—at least once in each column. (A sample for the "Congregation" column might read: pastor—Rev. Perez; teachers—Mrs. Li; leaders—my dad; choir members—me; worshipers—me; financial contributors—me. A sample for the "Friends" column might read: encourager—Sara; activity planner—me; the smart one—Connie [Everyone calls her with homework questions]; good listener—me and Dave; driver—Stu [He's the only one with his license *and* a car]; peacemaker—Sara.) Note that these functions and roles need not be the equivalent of spiritual gifts or service roles found in Scripture.

Closing Prayer

Have each young person think of one thing they do well and write down their answer. Have them pray in their small groups for ways they can serve God with that talent.

1. What does Paul mean when he calls himself a prisoner for the Lord?

5. Do you contribute to the unity or the division of the group? How?

2. How do you live a life worthy of the calling you have received to be one of God's children?

6. In verse 7, Paul describes grace apportioned by Christ for each one of us. What does that mean?

Working Together

3. What is the unity of the Spirit and how do we keep it?

7. In verse 11, Paul lists several ways people are called to serve Christ. What is the purpose of these various jobs?

4. How do the youth in your congregation try to keep the unity of the Spirit?

8. According to Paul what is the problem when a Christian community is not held close together?

What about You?

Congregation	Youth Ministry	Family	Friends

Solid Truth

Gifts of Grace

Romans 6:1–14

Study Outline

Opening Activity

Welcome the students. Lead the group in the following prayer: "Loving Father, we know we live in a sinful world. In a very real way sin touches our lives on a daily basis. When we rely on our own power, we find ourselves going against Your will. We rejoice that You forgive our sins. Thanks for sending Your Son, Jesus, to make that possible. Today, help us, through the power of the Holy Spirit, to discover how You touch our lives every day with that Good News. In Jesus' name we ask it. Amen."

Worthwhile Words

Before class gather several newsmagazines or newspapers, scissors, paper, and glue.

Distribute some of the magazines or newspapers and a sheet of paper to each student. Ask the students check the magazines for quotations from people. Instruct them to cut out interesting quotes and glue them to their sheet of paper. Statements from politicians, sports figures, entertainers, or other famous people would be appropriate. Give the students 10 minutes to complete the activity.

When time is up, call the students together. Invite volunteers to share some of the quotations they have found.

Then ask a volunteer to read aloud Genesis 1:1–3. Point out that God's Word had great power. He spoke and things happened—literally. The words of humans may make the news today or this week, but God's

Focus

One of God's great gifts to us is the forgiveness of sins. Because of Jesus's sacrificial suffering on the cross the debt has been paid, our sins are forgiven. Our forgiveness comes to us through the means of grace. Each time we hear the Good News of the Gospel, we hear an announcement of our forgiveness. On a daily basis God touches our lives through Baptism and the Lord's Supper. Both Sacraments have been commanded by Christ. Each carries with it the forgiveness of sins. They give young people a reason to celebrate even in a sin-filled world.

Objectives

Through the power of God's Word students will

1. identify the ways in which the Holy Spirit communicates the Good News of the forgiveness of sins to us;

2. connect Christ's suffering and death on the cross with Baptism and the Lord's Supper;

3. apply the forgiveness of sins to their specific daily encounters with sin.

It may be that some students in your class are not yet baptized. Be sensitive to this as you teach the lesson. You may wish to follow the pattern set in the lesson text as it talks about the benefits of Baptism in a way that can be past or future ("When we are baptized" rather than "when we were baptized").

You may also wish to have a private conversation with students who are not yet baptized and refer them to your pastor to discuss this matter.

What Is a Sacrament?

A sacrament is a sacred act through which God touches the lives of His people that

- has been commanded by God in the clear words of Scripture (see Matthew 28:19–20; Acts 2:39 and 22:16; and Luke 22:19–20);
- gives the forgiveness of sins earned by Christ;
- makes use of visible elements.

In Baptism the visible element is the water. In the Lord's Supper the visible elements are the bread and wine through which we receive the body and blood of Christ. Together with God's Word these Sacraments are frequently called means of grace, for they bring God's Good News of forgiveness and new life through Christ.

words have stood the text of time. Ask another student to read aloud Matthew 3:17. Remind the students that these were God's words of approval for the ministry His Son, Jesus, was about to undertake—teaching God's Word of salvation, demonstrating God's power through healing, living the life of perfect obedience and dying the death that would pay for the sins of the whole world. The words of Jesus are worth listening to and heeding, the Father says. When Jesus speaks we listen.

Studying the Word

Use both of these activities.

The Gift of Grace

If your class is large, divide it into small groups of 3–5 students. Provide the students with paper and pencils or pens. Instruct the groups to select one person to read Romans 6:1–14, pausing after verses 4, 7, and 10. The other students will follow along in their Bibles. At each pause they should review what they have heard and record notes on their paper. For example, a note for Romans 6:1–4 might read, "At the time of Baptism the sin in us is put to death. In its place we have a new life won for us by Jesus on the cross." Allow about 10 minutes for the students to complete the task.

When time is up, call the class together. Instruct them to close their Bibles and put away their notes. Say, "I am going to challenge you to recall what you just read. I am going to read an incomplete statement. In your small group you are to decide how the sentence might be completed. You'll have 30 seconds to respond."

Read each of the statements below, giving the students 30 seconds to answer.

1. Through Baptism we are dead to sin but ... (alive in Christ.)
2. Our old self was put to death so ... (we might have new life.)
3. We are no longer slaves to sin, so ... (we are free to serve God and others.)
4. Don't let sin reign over you or ... (follow evil desires.)
5. Do not use your body for evil things ... (use it to serve God.)
6. Before your Baptism sin was your master, but ... (under grace, God is your Master.)

Conclude by pointing out that God has given us the gift of salvation through the suffering, death, and resurrection of Jesus. For those who do not yet have faith, Baptism gives the Holy Spirit and adds that person to God's family. In the Sacrament of Holy Baptism, God also renews us daily as we remember our sins and trust in Him for forgiveness. Each morning we can begin the day knowing God has given us a fresh start. Likewise, the Sacrament of Holy Communion reminds us of His suffering and death and shares with us the forgiveness of sins He won for us on the cross.

Two Sacraments, One Gift

Divide the class into two equal groups. If you have 15 or more students in your class, split the class into four groups and assign each of the passages to two groups. Distribute copies of Resource Page 10A.

Invite the students to compare the two special gifts God has given His church in the Sacraments of Holy Baptism and the Lord's Supper/Holy Communion. Assign one group to complete the Baptism column on the resource page and the other group to complete the column for the Lord's Supper. Each group is to look up the Scripture references listed under that Sacrament and then answer the questions. Allow 10 minutes for this assignment.

Then call the groups together. Give each the opportunity to share their responses. Appropriate responses include:

Baptism: Instituted by Jesus; physical element—water; gift—forgiveness of sins.

Holy Communion: Instituted by Jesus; physical elements—body and blood of Christ under the bread and wine; gift—forgiveness of sins.

Conclude by telling the students that while both Sacraments bring the same gift, the forgiveness of sins, and both show God's love for us, they differ in some ways. For many, Baptism is a rite of initiation, a beginning of faith. For some it is the affirmation of the faith that is already theirs through the Word. It always precedes reception of the Lord's Supper.

The Lord's Supper is a meal, an ongoing source of spiritual nourishment for the Christian. In it we receive the body and blood of Christ for the strengthening of our faith as well as the forgiveness of sins. Two Sacraments, one gift, but two unique opportunities to grow in faith.

Applying the Word

Choose one of the activities that follow, but not both, unless you have extra time.

God's Special Servant

Distribute copies of Resource Page 10B, the fictional story of a woman who celebrated God's forgiveness each day as she remembered her Baptism. Recruit a volunteer to read the story aloud. Then discuss the story, using the following questions:

1. Mrs. Murphy made her Baptism and the gift of forgiveness of sins a focal point in her life. How did she respond to that gift on a daily basis? (Through her many acts of service in the church and community.)

2. What can baptized Christians do each day to remember their Baptism? (Encourage the students to be creative—posting things on the wall, on the bathroom mirror, or in the shower; a "wake-up" invocation using the words of the baptismal service, "In the name

Symbols of Salvation

As an alternative to writing responses on Resource Page 10A, assign one or more passages to each student and invite each student to design a symbol that will convey the message of each passage. Allow the students about 10 minutes to complete the assignment.

As students complete their symbols, mount them to the wall for everyone to see. Give each student the opportunity to explain their sketch.

of the Father, Son, and Holy Spirit;" creating wallet-sized reproduction of our Baptism certificates.)

3. In what ways can or do we show our membership in God's family each day? (Answers will vary.)

Conclude by reminding the students that, while Baptism is a one-time event, its benefits last a lifetime. Baptism brings with it a daily renewal as we celebrate the fact that our sins have been washed away. Because of Baptism, we can live each day joyfully and serve others as we give honor and glory to Jesus Christ our Savior.

Action Plan

Provide each student with paper and a pen or pencil. Introduce this activity by saying, "Through the waters of Baptism God makes us, or confirms us as, members of His family and calls us to a life of service. With the Spirit's help we can develop an action plan to guide our service. In order to develop such a plan, across the top of your paper write 'As a Baptized Child of God I promise to …' Then list (1) the things you plan to do to remind yourself each day of your Baptism and (2) the things you hope to do as you reflect Jesus Christ, who lives in you through faith as a result of your Baptism."

(Examples for the first item could include: Have my Baptismal Certificate framed and mounted in my room, have personal devotions each day, and remember my Baptism every time I pass a drinking fountain. Examples of item 2: be more sensitive to the needs of people about me, volunteer at the local hospital or neighborhood activity center, spend more time with a younger brother or sister.)

Give the students 10–15 minutes to complete this activity. Since an action plan is a personal document do not ask the students to share what they have written. As you monitor the students, commend them for both their creativity and desire to serve God.

Closing Prayer

Close the session by leading the class in the following prayer.

"Loving Father, thank You for the blessings You give through the washing of Holy Baptism to those who are part of Your family. Thank You as well for the gift of Holy Communion and the forgiveness of sins Christians receive through it. May that Good News motivate us to live each day as Your servants. Through the power of Your Spirit enable us to grow in our faith and service. In Jesus' name we pray. Amen."

This activity may not be appropriate for students that are not yet baptized. Use your discretion.

80

Two Sacraments, One Gift

	Baptism	The Lord's Supper
1. Where is it commanded?	John 3:5 Matthew 28:19–20 Acts 2:38–39	Matthew 26:26–28 Luke 22:19–20
2. By whom?		
3. What are the physical elements?		
4. What gifts or benefits are received?		

Solid Truth

Mrs. Murphy's Secret

For as long as anyone could remember, Mrs. Murphy had been a member of Trinity Church. Everyone knew her because it was hard to miss her. You name an activity and she was in the middle of it. Few people could recall meeting her husband. He had died at a young age, leaving her a widow. Since she had no children of her own, the children at church became her family.

Most of the kids remembered her best as the third-grade Sunday school teacher. Even after you had graduated from her class you had to stop by for a hug. When it was vacation Bible school time, the kids loved her chocolate chip cookies. She also dedicated herself to serving others. She sang in the choir, volunteered in the church office, and was new-member chairman for the women's missionary league. She supervised the altar guild and made banners for special occasions. Her spaghetti casserole was always a hit at the church potluck suppers.

Whenever anyone would compliment her on her kindness and hard work she would comment, "Jesus gave His life for me. I don't mind giving part of my time for Him. "The kids in her Sunday school class always detected a special feeling when Mrs. Murphy talked about Baptism. She tried to make each Baptism special by presenting their parents with a Baptism banner. Instead of sending her students' birthday cards, she would send cards on the child's Baptism "birthday."

All of that came to a sudden end. It was appropriate that Mrs. Murphy died at church. She was in the office updating membership records when she had a heart attack. She was dead even before the paramedics arrived. There was nothing anyone could do.

At her funeral the kids from the Sunday school all sat together. Following the service, Pastor Berg called all the kids and invited them to come to Mrs. Murphy's home. The next day the kids assembled in her living room. The room seemed somehow empty without Mrs. Murphy's presence.

"There is something very special that Mrs. Murphy wanted you to know," Pastor Berg began. He led them into her bedroom. There on the wall at the foot of her bed was hung her baptismal certificate. It was beautifully hand-lettered and illustrated in ink drawings of several colors, now faded somewhat because of the years. The frame was highly polished wood.

"This is the first thing Mrs. Murphy would see each morning when she got up," the pastor reported. "She remembered the forgiveness and new life that God gave her in Baptism. That was always her motivation. She made me promise to share that with you. Her prayer was that you would have that same motivation. As a child of God, you can begin each day knowing you are forgiven. That is a reason to celebrate and to serve others. That's the way Mrs. Murphy lived. She hoped you would do the same."

Holy Living

John 15:1–8

Study Outline

Activity	Time Suggested	Materials Needed
Opening Activities		
Introduction and Prayer	5 minutes	A small, bouncy ball
The Chains of Sin	10 minutes	Construction paper; tape; markers
Studying the Word		
Fruitful Disciples	15 minutes	Bibles; copies of Resource Page 11
Applying the Word		
Bearing Fruit	15 minutes	Pictures of service activities
Closing Activity and Prayer	10 minutes	Copies of the litany on page 87

Opening Activities

Introduction and Prayer

Take a ball and bounce it on the floor. Then throw it in the air. Point out that whenever you throw the ball down it bounces up, and whenever you toss it up it comes down. Ask them why that happens. (In both cases, "laws of nature" are at work, though the reactive process of the bounce is more complicated than the simple application of gravity to the tossed ball.) Point out that similar "natural laws" are at work in our lives of Christian faith. Ephesians 2:10 says that we were "created in Christ Jesus to do good works." This study will explore how the Holy Spirit makes that happen more and more in the lives of God's people.

Then lead the students in this prayer: "Dear Lord, today is a good day, and we thank and praise You for it. As we study Your Word today, please guide us. May Your Holy Spirit bless our time and allow Your Word to bear fruit in our lives. In Jesus' name we ask it. Amen."

The Chains of Sin

Give the students several strips of black construction paper, white crayons or chalk, and clear tape (in a pinch, any kind and color of paper and any markers will do). Have the students write on each strip a name or description of a sin they see in their lives or in the world around them. As they work, remind them of implications of the God's commandments for the world: "All have sinned and fall short of the glory of God" (Romans 3:23), "Whoever keeps the whole law and yet

Focus

As the Holy Spirit works faith in us, we are freed from the guilt and power of sin. The Good News of forgiveness creates in us new life that willingly serves God and acts in ways pleasing to Him. Such spiritual fruit is the natural product of branches attached to the life-giving Vine—Jesus Christ. Fruit does not grow on branches are separated from the Vine. Neither does the fruit create the branch's connection with the Vine. Young people can rejoice that their holy living is not a matter of personal effort and self-discipline apart from God's grace, but a product of that grace.

Objectives

Through the power of God's Word, students will

1. see that holy living follows the forgiveness of sins in the Christian life, not the other way around;
2. identify the means by which good works take place in the lives of Christians;
3. celebrate the freedom from sin and the opportunities for service that the Spirit provides.

stumbles at just one point is guilty of breaking all of it" (James 2:10), and "The wages of sin is death, but the gift of God is eternal life in Christ Jesus our Lord" (Romans 6:23).

Have each student tape his or her strips into a chain. Then ask the whole group to join their chains together into one big chain. Display the chain on the floor, a chair, or on the wall for the rest of this study. (It will be used during the closing.)

Studying the Word
Fruitful Disciples

It may be helpful to consult an encyclopedia or other reference book for details about the various vine-tending techniques in John 15. See, for example, entries under <u>grape</u>.

Hand out Resource Page 11. If you have a large class, you may wish to break into groups of six to eight and assign someone to lead the group through the activity. If you do this, gather the small groups together into one large group to review what they discovered.

Have the students read John 15:1–8, 16–17. Then discuss, or have the small groups discuss, the chart and questions. Students may complete the chart as follows:

- Gardener (verse 1)—God the Father
- Vine (verse 1)—Jesus Christ
- Branch (verse 4)—a disciple, a follower of Jesus
- Cuts off (verses 2, 6)—God will judge the unbelievers, those who produce no fruit. They will be judged for their unbelief, not their lack of fruit. The fruit is only a symptom of faith.
- Prunes (verses 2–3)—God works in the lives of believers to keep them closely attached to life-giving Vine, Jesus Christ, and productive disciples who bear the fruit of faith.
- Fruit (verses 4, 8, 16)—The good works and holy living of the disciple. Two particular ones mentioned in John 15 are prayer (asking for God's blessings for ourselves and others—verses 7, 16b) and love (verse 12).

Appropriate replies to the questions include the following:

1. What is the Gardener's purpose for the vineyard? What does He expect will happen? (God intends the disciple to produce fruit, good works and Christian living. "Showing yourself to be my disciples" [verse 8] and "Fruit that will last" [verse 16] give an outreach slant to our works. Leading others to see Jesus Christ as their Vine is a fruit that will last forever.)

2. How were the disciples made "clean," that is "pruned"? (Verse 3 says the disciples were made clean by Jesus' word—God shows us our sin, offers us free and full forgiveness, and gives us the power to resist sin and to live lives of service to Him.)

3. The Gardener provides the labor; the Vine provides the "life." What does the disciples' effort produce? (Nothing! Apart from the Vine, the branch is incapable of producing fruit of any kind. Our good works are not really ours [they are God's work in us], they are not really "good" [they do not make us good in God's eyes; that is the

work of Jesus], and they are not really work [they flow naturally from us by God's grace without effort on our part].)

4. What kind of fruit is your Gardener producing in you? (Answers will vary. Help every student to see God at work in him or her in some way.)

Applying the Word

Bearing Fruit

Find a half dozen pictures of people of any age doing works of service: repairing a house, volunteering in a hospital, tutoring children or teaching in a Christian-education class, doing yard work, picking up trash, or helping an elderly person are all possibilities.

Display or pass around the pictures. Then ask the students to identify what is taking place in each picture.(Volunteer acts of service and help to others. Make sure they identify the type of activity and setting of each picture.) Then as why they think the people pictured might be doing the activity? (Any guess by the students is fine here. Make the point that you cannot tell what their motivation is just from the picture. Although we may assume that these are Christians involved in service, acting out their faith, this may not be so for every situation depicted. Some of the youth pictured may not believe in Jesus. They may be of another religion, such as Muslim, Buddhist, or Jewish. Or they may be youth who are not part of any religion, and are volunteering through school or work activities, or even as community service ordered by a court of law.)

Remind the students that the Bible's message is clear: our acts of service as Christians result from Christ at work in us through the Holy Spirit. These actions point to God at work in us, but they do not gain us any favor with God in regard to our salvation.

Remind the students that John 15 described both living, fruitful branches and withered, fruitless ones. Ask again what caused the difference between them. ("Remaining in Christ"—that is, staying closely connected to Him and relying on His grace for all things.)

Then ask, "What are some specific ways we are brought into connection with Jesus and God's Word?" (Here, a good discussion can be generated about how worship and the Sacraments refresh and empower us, how reading and meditating on God's Word can be used by the Spirit to strengthen our faith, the importance of praying for others, and how gathering with other Christians regularly for fellowship can be uplifting and edifying. Use as much or as little time as you have available to bring out these points. Share your personal stories about being strengthened by the Holy Spirit through the Word, the Lord's Supper, seeing your child baptized or confirmed and remembering your own experiences, being encouraged by a Christian brother or sister, or other faith-enriching experiences you have had.)

Remind the students that we occasionally fail to bear fruit, fail to act out our faith, and fail to always do what God desires. These are the

A leafy branch and a dry, dead one might be useful objects to use during discussion of the Bible verses. Depending on the season, a branch or vegetable stalk with fruit attached might also be available.

times when we benefit greatly from God's grace. We can repent, ask for forgiveness, trust in God's grace to heal us and make us more obedient, and rely on the Spirit to motivate us to live out Christ's love in us every day. Emphasize to the students that no matter what has happened in the past, no matter how poorly one feels they have acted out their faith, today forgiveness is available through Christ and the power to do the will of God is promised through the Holy Spirit acting in their lives.

Help the students see that today is a new day, and they can live their new life in Christ through the power of the Spirit in them right now. Have the students brainstorm a list of activities they could be involved with today, this week, this month, and this year to bear the fruit of Christ's love in their lives. It may be something they do as individuals, or as a group. It may be a small thing like mowing an elderly neighbor's yard or helping their family with shopping. Or it may be something larger like organizing a community cleanup or house repair day for the poor.

Lead the students to pick from this list things they would enjoy doing. Encourage them to pursue it! Maybe your class could organize something they could do as a group, either as a one-time activity or an ongoing service. Maybe its something they do for the congregation, or for the community or a specific person. If your congregation's youth ministry has scheduled a servant event or short-term mission trip in the future, refer to it as a great opportunity to put their faith into action and live according to Christ's love within them.

Closing Activity and Prayer

For this closing you will need the chain the students made earlier. Ask for a volunteer to be "chained" with it. Put them in the center of the group to do this. Remind the students how sin keeps us from doing God's will. Distribute copies of the litany on the following page and say it together. You may want to serve as leader, or you may want a student to read the leader sections.

Now have the person in chains break out of them. Clap and shout to celebrate this symbol of our sin having no hold on us! Share a prayer of thanks and praise to God for His grace and mercy. The following prayer could be used.

"Dear Lord, we thank You for Your love for us. We thank You for Your mercy upon us. Strengthen and empower us this day, and every day, to lead holy lives and do the righteous acts of love You will us to do through the power of the Holy Spirit in our lives and the love we have in Christ Jesus. We ask this in His name. Amen."

Leader: Lord, we come to You today knowing You love us.

Group 1: You loved us by sending Your Son to die for our sins.

Group 2: *You loved us by sending Your Spirit to be part of our lives day-in and day-out.*

Leader: You love us now, because You listen to our prayer.

Group 1: Lord, we confess that we do not always live out the faith You have given us.

Group 2: *We confess we do not always act out of love for You.*

All: But we trust in Your mercy and grace!

Leader: Listen to His Word, "In Him we have redemption through His blood, the forgiveness of sins, in accordance with the riches of God's grace." (Ephesians 1:7)

All: Praise God for His goodness and mercy!

Fruitful Disciples

In John 15, Jesus uses the analogy of a vineyard to illustrate the life of discipleship. Complete the chart below, listing for each term in the vine column its the counterpart in our lives as disciples. Then respond to the questions that follow.

Vine	Our Life
Gardener (verse 1)	
Vine (verse 1)	
Branch (verse 4)	
Cuts off (verses 2 and 6)	
Prunes (verses 2 and 3)	
Fruit (verses 4, 8, and 16)	

1. What is the Gardener's purpose for the vineyard? What does He expect will happen?

2. How were the disciples made "clean"? (The Greek word also means "pruned"—that is, the disciples had already been pruned and made fruitful. How?)

3. Growing grapes is a labor-intensive activity. The vinedresser (called a gardener in Jesus' story) plants rootstock, grafts on branches to create hybrid varieties of grapes and control the kind and character of the fruit, prunes the branches to guide the growth of the fruit, and replaces unproductive branches with new grafts. The gardener provides the labor, the vine—with its roots in the soil—provides the "life." What does this say about the disciples' ability to produce the fruit of good works? (See especially verse 16.)

4. What kind of fruit is your Gardener producing in you?

The End

Romans 8:28–39

Study Outline

Activity	Time Suggested	Materials Needed
Opening Activity (Choose one activity in addition to prayer)		
Prayer	2 minutes	
Confidence or Fear?	10 minutes	
Take a Chance	10 minutes	Deck of cards or dice (optional)
Studying the Word		
Important Questions, Important Answers	20 minutes	Copies of Resource Page 12A; Bibles (Optional: copies of Resource Page 12C)
Applying the Word (Choose one)		
Reasons for Confidence	15 minutes	Newsprint or marker board and markers; Bibles
Letter to a Friend	20 minutes	Copies of Resource Page 12B
Closing Prayer	5 minutes	

Opening Activity

Prayer

Begin by leading the students in a prayer such as the following:

"Heavenly Father, You have blessed us in every way, meeting our material needs, giving us faith in Christ, and inviting us to serve You. Help us to face the future, whatever it may bring, with confidence, knowing that it too is in Your hands. In Jesus' name we pray. Amen."

Confidence or Fear?

Use this activity or the next one, but not both, unless you have extra time.

Challenge the students to think of situations where knowing the outcome—especially knowing that the outcome would be positive—would make a big difference in how we would approach them. As they respond, write their suggestions on newsprint or on the board and discuss the difference knowing the outcome would make. Some possible situations might be as follows:

• facing major surgery
• deciding whether to move or change careers
• playing a difficult opponent in the sport of your choice
• performing in a recital

Focus

"How will it end?" Those caught in the quicksand of doubt and despair that results from postmodern thinking may see little reason for hope. The Holy Spirit through the Gospel creates faith and gives great hope. Through the Gospel we can be sure of our place among those to whom God has promised eternal life. Our own death, Christ's second coming, the final judgment, and the end of the world are not causes for despair when we know "the end of the story." The God who created and loves us, who redeemed us by His blood on the cross, and who calls us to faith will greet us as dearly loved children and welcome us home for all eternity.

Objectives

Through the power of God's Word, students will

1. identify the reason for certain hope of eternal life;
2. express confidence that through faith they will be with God in a new heaven and a new earth at the end of their days;
3. share a testimony of their Christian faith with others.

89

In each case, help the students to see that knowing ahead of time that the outcome would be success can produce great confidence, while uncertainty often creates fear. Both the confidence and the fear can affect not only the participant's feelings, but also his or her actions. (This study focuses on such *positive* foreknowledge. Sometimes knowing the outcome could lead to arrogance, risk-taking, or other negative behaviors. Knowing that we will fail could lead to despair. While these are both true statements, they are not the direction of the study. You need not emphasize them.)

Wrap up this section by saying something such as, "Knowing how something is going to turn out makes a world of difference in how you approach it. If you are sure you will win, you are confident and looking forward to the event. If you are doubtful, there is often fear and intimidation. When it comes to your life with God, how are things going? Is your life characterized more by confidence or fear? Today we want to look at life's outcome and see how that affects us in our road through life."

Take a Chance

Use this activity or the previous one, but not both, unless you have extra time.

Challenge the students to a "game of chance." You can use dice, a deck of cards, or just the familiar "pick a number between 1 and ..." game. You will not use any wagers and, by design, the game will not involve any "chance."

Ask the students how willing they would be to play a game of chance if they have a "normal" chance to win. (Guessing one card in a deck has "1 in 52" odds; odds for guessing the total of two dice vary from "1 in 36" to "1 in 6;" for "pick a number," the number of choices determines the odds. Gauge their response. Perhaps a few will be very willing, others obviously reluctant.

Then ask how their attitude would change if they were guaranteed better odds by, say, picking a black card, rolling an even number, or "picking the correct number between 1 and 2." (Each has odds of "1 in 2.") The students will likely be more enthusiastic as their chance of winning increases.

Ask the students how the improved chance of a good outcome affects their attitude about the game and why. How might it affect their participation in the game? Point out that the "game of life" for some people results in frustration, doubt, and hopelessness. They don't know how things will turn out. God's people have hope, because we know how the game ends: in our favor. This study is about that kind of hope and how it changes our daily lives.

Studying the Word
Important Questions, Important Answers

Ask the students what they think people believe, or what other people might say, about what will happen at the end of their earthly existence. Do their friends generally accept the reality of heaven and hell? Point out that for many people, eternal life is in doubt. They have no doubts about what they want to be, where they want to live, how many kids they want to have—but when it comes to the most critical question concerning their lives, they're not sure of the answer. In Romans 8:28–39 the apostle Paul lays out why and how we can be sure of the answer to the questions: "Am I going to heaven?" and "How can I be sure?"

Distribute copies of Resource Page 12A and have the students find Romans 8. Direct them to respond to the questions on the resource page, working alone, in pairs, or in small groups.

Allow the students about 10 minutes to work on the questions. Then invite individuals to respond to each of them. Use the comments below to clarify and expand on their answers.

Verse 31—"If God is for us, who can be against us?"

Answer: No one of any significance.

Who is often "against" you?

Answer: The students responses will vary but may include classmates, parents, or employers.

How does knowing that God is "for you" help?

Answer: God will provide the encouragement we need in tough times, the support of friends and others, and the support of His Word. He will not let enemies overcome us.

Verse 32—"How will He not … give us all things?"

Answer: Yes, He has and will give us every good thing we have.

What is included in "all things"?

Answer: Everything we need to live a joyful life in Christ.

What is the proof that God is for us?

Answer: He did not spare His own Son.

Verses 33, 34—"Who will bring any charge …? Who is he that condemns?"

Answer: No one has the right or power to condemn us.

What kind of charges is Paul talking about?

Answer: Accusations that we have sinned, offended God in any. Though we are, indeed, guilty of such charges, we have an "iron clad" defense against them.

What is our defense against the charges?

Answer: God has chosen us in love, He justifies us through the work of His Son Jesus Christ, who kept the Law perfectly on our behalf.

Verse 35—"Who shall separate us from the love of Christ? Shall

An Option

For a longer session, or if you have a large class, use the optional Resource Page 12C, "What Do You Say?" Divide the students into groups of four or five and instruct them to read the story and answer the questions. After about 10 minutes ask volunteers to share what their group decided and why.

trouble or hardship or persecution or famine or nakedness or danger or sword?"

Answer: No one and nothing, says Paul, can separate us from God's love.

What things in people's lives today might seem to separate them from God's love?

Answer: There are many possible responses. Examples include poor health, bad luck, loneliness, sins they have committed, a belief that they are unworthy of God's love.

Verse 31—"What, then shall we say in response to this?"

Answer: Paul's answer is only implied, but surely it must be, "Awesome! Hallelujah! Our God is great!"

After reviewing these responses, point out to the students that not everyone experiences the reality of God's love and the certainty of eternal life with Him. Some never hear about God's love in Jesus Christ. Some hear, but choose instead to live under the Law, seeking to make their own way. (Studies 4 and 8 show the impossibility of "saving ourselves.") God has given us His Word, placed faith in our hearts through the Gospel, and promises us His eternal love.

Applying the Word
Reasons for Confidence

Use this activity or the one that follows, but not both, unless you have extra time.

Write on the marker board or newsprint the words, "Reasons for Confidence." Ask your class to sum up your discussion of the Romans passage by listing reasons they can be confident of God's love for them and that they will be with Him when the end comes. Some ideas to get them started—God chooses us based on His love for us, not on who we are or what we have done; God gives us faith and salvation as free gifts; God has given Jesus as proof of His love; God will never condemn us.

Then direct your class into groups of twos and threes. (In a small class you can do this activity as a group.) Ask, "When, for you, is it the most difficult to believe that Jesus loves you—that nothing can separate you from His love? In your groups share the times you find it hardest to rely on God's promise of unconditional love." (An example might be, "When I am angry at my parents it's hard for me to pray or feel God's presence." or "When I knowingly commit a sin, I know God knows but I still don't want to confess it to anyone. It feels like God is a long way off waiting for me to make up for it.")

Allow about five minutes for sharing in groups (or for personal reflection). Then ask, "What Bible verse or information from our study might help you realize God's never ending love for you, even in those times?" Allow sharing in the small groups or invite individuals to share their responses.

If this activity will challenge the trust level among the students and make some feel awkward, consider having the students write those situations where they find it hardest to rely on God's promise of love in all circumstances. Assure them that their responses are for personal reflection and that they will not have to share them.

Encourage them to pull some ideas from the "Reasons for Confidence" list and personalize them. They can also help each other with suggestions if someone is struggling to make the connection. For example, a student might share, "Even when I willingly commit a sin, I can remember that my sin doesn't diminish God's love for me. Because of Jesus' suffering and death, God does not see my sin, but Jesus in my place. This will help me to confess and rely on His strength to straighten things out."

Letter to a Friend

Use this activity or the previous one, but not both, unless you have extra time.

Distribute copies of Resource Page 12B. Invite the students to think about someone they might share their faith with. Tell them to write a letter to that person, sharing what they believe about heaven and the end of life on this earth. Encourage them to share that they have been saved by grace through faith and to tell why they have hope in this life based on God's unconditional love for them.

You might use this letter as an example for your group:

> Dear Mark,
>
> In Bible study recently, someone asked me what I believe about heaven. Was I confident of my place in heaven and why? The answer is pretty simple. It's because God chose me. I didn't do anything, He just chose me. I know this because in His Word it says that Jesus died that the whole world might be saved. I struggle a lot. But this same God promised me that no matter what, nothing could separate His love from me. In my best days He loves me. In my worst days He loves me. Each day for me is a new start because of Him. I just wanted to let you know why I have hope in God.
>
> If you'd like to know more, I'd love to talk to you about it.
>
> Your friend, Sarah.

Closing Prayer

Close with a time of prayer. You can help your students to pray for one another by using the following format:

"Dear God, thank You for Your great love for (student on right, left etc.). Please help (that student's name) to know Your love and live each day in Your grace. Show (that student's name) someone with whom to share the Good News of Your love for the whole world. In Jesus' name I ask it. Amen."

If your class is not used to praying aloud for one another, distribute a printed form with the suggested wording of the prayer, so that students can just fill in the blanks. Direct the students into pairs. Have them share with each other some ways that they are thankful for God's love. Have them also name someone that they might witness to about their own faith and how God's love has made a difference in their lives. The information can be used to complete the form, which is then used for prayer.

Important Questions, Important Answers

The apostle Paul raises some really important questions in Romans 8—questions that have really important answers. Review Romans 8 and write the responses Paul intends.

Verse 31—"If God is for us, who can be against us?"

Answer: _____

_____

Who is often "against" you?

Answer: _____

How does knowing that God is "for you" help?

Answer: _____

Verse 32—"How will He not ... give us all things?"

Answer: _____

What is included in "all things"?

Answer: _____

What is the proof that God is for us?

Answer: _____

_____

Verses 33, 34—"Who will bring any charge ...? Who is he that condemns?"

Answer: _____

_____

What kind of charges is Paul talking about?

Answer: _____

_____

What is our defense against the charges?

Answer: _____

_____

Verse 35—"Who shall separate us from the love of Christ? Shall trouble or hardship or persecution or famine or nakedness or danger or sword?"

Answer: _____

What things in people's lives today might seem to separate them from God's love?

Answer: _____

_____

Verse 31—"What, then shall we say in response to this?"

Answer: _____

_____

Letter to a Friend

Dear _____

Solid Truth

What Do You Say?

Your friend Hank is a great guy. He is a fairly good student, tries hard to be helpful and nice to people and goes out of his way to obey his parents. Recently he has started coming to some of your church activities and seems to be genuinely interested in Christianity. He just keeps getting stuck on Baptism and what it means to "die to yourself and live for Christ."

As you leave school one day you see a crowd gathered around someone lying in the street. You recognize that person as Hank, and you can tell he's been hit by a car. You run over and notice that he looks pretty bad, like he might not make it. He reaches out to you and says, "I'm really scared. I've tried to be good. I've never killed anyone or stolen anything. Recently, I've heard about Jesus at your church. But I just don't know if I'm good enough, if I believe strong enough. I still have questions. If I don't make it, will I go to heaven?" From the looks of things, you may only have a few minutes. And no, your pastor is not around. What do you say? What could you say that could give him absolute assurance that he would be with God forever?

(Here are a few verses to help you out if you're stuck: John 1:12; John 3:16–17; John 14:1–3; Romans 10:8–13; 1 John 5:11–13.)

What could you share from your own life, how Jesus has saved you, that might help Hank understand?